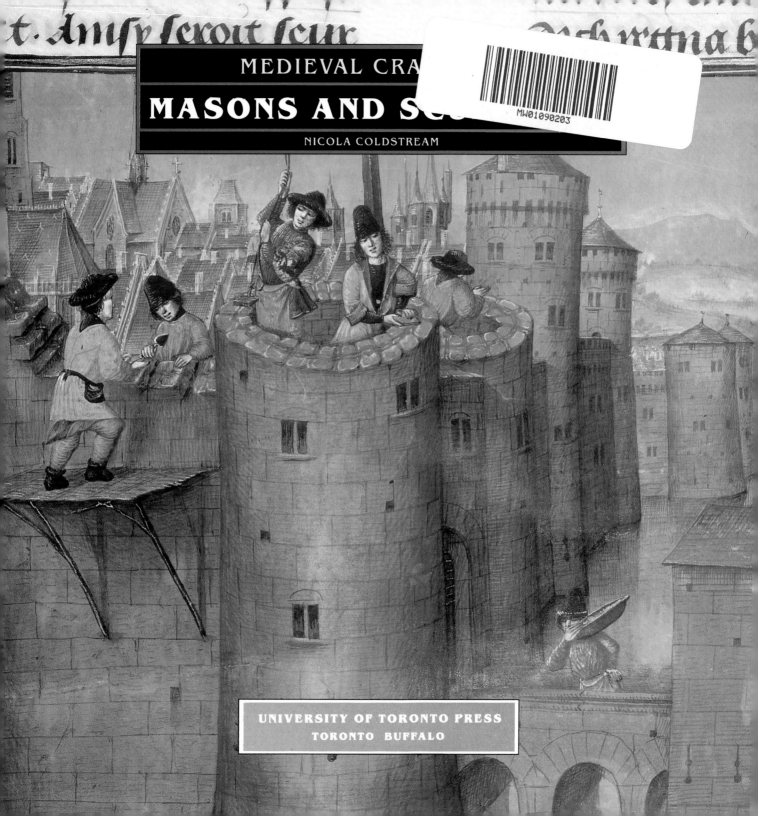

MEDIEVAL CRA
MASONS AND S

NICOLA COLDSTREAM

UNIVERSITY OF TORONTO PRESS
TORONTO BUFFALO

Reprinted 1998

ISBN 0-8020-6916-9

Designed and set on Ventura
in Palatino by Roger Davies,
The Green Street Press.

Printed and bound in Hong
Kong.

Front cover Masons using trowels to mortar stone, hammers and chisels to cut stone, and set squares to measure stone. See fig. 47.

Back cover A fifteenth-century miniature showing the building of the Tower of Babel. See fig. 6.

Title page As well as using scaffolding platforms, masons would use the finished walls as platforms from which to carry on their work.

This page Harlech Castle, one of the 'ring of castles' built in Snowdonia by Edward II in the late thirteenth century. A building programme on this scale needed an efficient central administration, and all major works were administered by specially appointed Clerks of the Works.

To my father, Charles Carr

Acknowledgements

A brief, compressed study of this kind owes more to the work of other scholars than can be recognised in a short bibliography. While preparing this book I have benefited particularly from the writings of Lon R. Shelby and Barbara Schock-Werner, and from the mouldings studies of Richard Morris. Peter Kidson kindly read the section on design, and pointed out to me many years ago that one did not need to be a mathematician to understand medieval systems of proportion. Finally, I am grateful to Celia Clear and Rachel Rogers of British Museum Press for their editorial help and cheerful efficiency over the smallest details, and to Susan Bird for drawing the text figures.

Contents

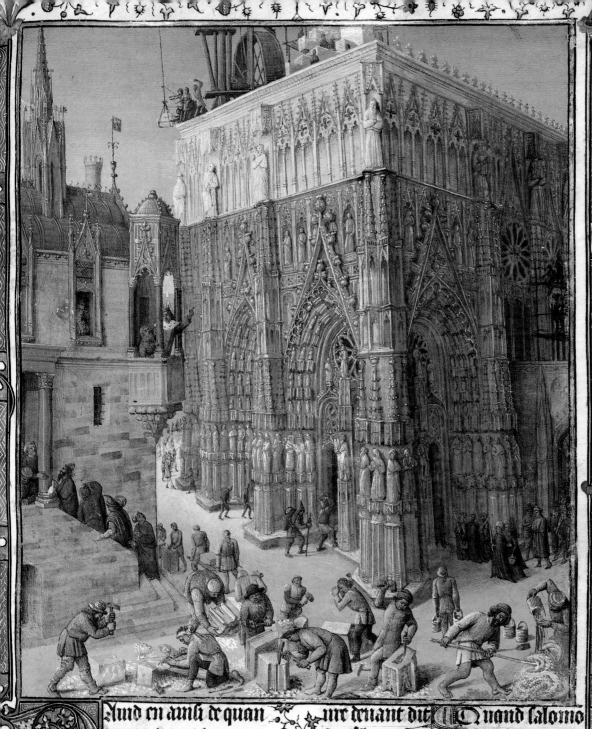

Auid en aulli de quan
tes uertus et de quants
biens il a este aucteur
a ceulr de sa ligniee. et
combien plam de grant aige il est

me deuant dit. Quand salomo
son filz: ancores ieune enfant eut
pris le royaume de son pere. et fu
assis ou siege royal. tout le peuple
solennelement fauoir. comme on

INTRODUCTION

The medieval mason has been, and to some extent still is, the subject of romantic myth. For many years an erroneous link was traced between medieval freemasons and the comparatively modern fraternity of Freemasons, but the medieval term 'freemason' means a mason who worked in freestone, that is, stone that could be carved with or against the grain without developing a fault; this has nothing to do with the adoption centuries later of certain masonic attributes for the rituals of a secret society. Other misconceptions are that medieval buildings were the work of monks, inspired amateurs driven by faith; or that so sophisticated a building as a Gothic cathedral could not have been designed by an anonymous, uneducated stonemason, but must have been the work of the scholarly clerical patrons.

Such confusions arise from the modern idea of an architect — promulgated from the fifteenth-century Italian Renaissance — as a scholar-designer, who draws up his design according to accepted principles and theories, and gives the scaled and annotated blueprints to the builder who actually executes the design. By contrast, the medieval architect, or master mason, was a very different being; he got his hands dirty. It was not in a studio that he was trained in design but on the building site. The word 'architect' was rarely used in the Middle Ages, the usual terms, *lathomus* or *caementarius*, indicating his association with quarries and the stone industry. In the eyes of the Church (a prominent building patron) the one true architect was God Himself, the architect of the universe, and mere men had to define themselves in other terms.

The master mason acted as contractor, engineer and designer, combining in his single person what would nowadays be the jobs of three, all with different training. A professional layman, he rose from the ranks of the journeymen masons and was never entirely detached from them. He was expected to turn his hand to any building work, however apparently demeaning. William Ramsay, for instance, was a leading fourteenth-century English mason who designed buildings for the king and for the cathedral authorities of London and Lichfield, yet at the Tower of London he had to do repairs and recrenellation, and at Windsor, where he worked briefly, he was 'first cutting mason', evidently required to work alongside the labour force. The separation of the art of design from the knowledge of how to build is a post-medieval development, and it is crucial to the understanding of how medieval buildings were designed and constructed to realise that the whole process was rooted in the practical tradition of the masons' craft.

Medieval building records begin seriously only from the eleventh century, with the great building boom that has lasted ever since. The art of masonry had been taken to a very high level by ancient civilisations, but in western Europe masonry skills declined with the Roman Empire, to revive only gradually from the ninth century. We know almost nothing about these early masons, but throughout the period covered by this book — the twelfth to

1 *Opposite* Fifteenth-century miniature of the Temple of Jerusalem from Flavius Josephus' *Jewish Antiquities*, illustrated by Jean Fouquet. The Temple, which Solomon ordered to be built (see I. Kings, vi), is here depicted as a Christian church. In the foreground masons and sculptors are carving mouldings and figures, while others hoist stones to the top of the building.

2 *Right* A page from the fourteenth-century *Holkham Bible Picture Book* showing God as architect of the universe, creating the world with a giant pair of compasses. Because He was regarded as the supreme architect the term was reserved for Him, and medieval architects were usually referred to as masons.

3 The Norman Castle and Cathedral of Durham. Buildings such as these were large public undertakings that dominated the lives of those living in their shadow.

the sixteenth centuries — there is plenty of evidence, although it is often patchy and indirect. Masons seem anonymous to us only because a critical account of the life and work of a medieval mason can scarcely ever be written, and because any great building could take from ten years to several generations to complete and can therefore rarely be ascribed to a single architect. Anonymous, however, masons were not.

Castles and great churches were built both for permanence and for the display of temporal or spiritual power. A great building enterprise, particularly if it were in a town, was a public event. A cathedral, rising in or at the edge of one of the main civic spaces of a city, was in a sense public property even if, as we shall see, the townspeople managed to avoid having to contribute to the costs of building. Local labour was employed at least for the unskilled work and, for all its inherent dangers, the building site was open to the curious. At Troyes Cathedral in France, for example, the authorities were obliged to cover unfinished masonry with briars to prevent children from climbing on it, and on at least one occasion selected citizens were consulted about building decisions by the bishop. Even though a complex building campaign involved a large number of

people — on the one side the patron and the administrative officials, and on the other the masons, carpenters, glaziers, plumbers and others who made up the labour force — it was the masons who played the principal role. They were the élite: there were far fewer of them on the payroll than the unskilled support workers. Responsible for every stage of the building process, from the design and setting out to the construction and decoration, they were constantly in the public eye. It is modern perceptions of their role, together with the fugitive nature of much of the evidence, that has caused them to vanish from our eyes, but in the pages that follow we shall try to discover who they were, how they organised their professional lives, and how they designed and built the castles and great churches that survive as testimony to their creative skills.

The evidence is varied, and as most of it dates from the later Middle Ages we have to be wary of generalising back into the earlier period; it is also tantalisingly incomplete, and much is still not understood. The masons themselves left many personal records — from contracts and building accounts to casual affirmations of their own sense of self-worth in tombstones, inscriptions, wills and portraits — from which we can gain some idea of their

4 Portrait bust of Hans von Burghausen, the architect of St Martin's at Landshut, Bavaria, which was placed in the church shortly after his death in 1432. He was the leading south German architect of his day, and the bust and epitaph listing the churches that he built reflect the esteem in which he was held.

5 The seal with the personal mark of Ulrich von Ensingen, master mason of Strasbourg Cathedral in the early fifteenth century. The mason's mark originated as an identification mark on cut stones, but it was adopted by many late medieval masons as a signature.

changing status and function. In late medieval Germany the mason's mark, which had originated as an identification mark on cut stones, was adopted by leading masters and their families as a form of personal signature, with variations added by younger generations rather as with coats of arms. The art and practice of masonry are expounded in sets of masons' regulations, the earliest of which survive from 1352 in York, and masons' ordinances, also from the fourteenth and fifteenth centuries, which sought to codify and control the trade. For buildings and the building process there are administrative accounts, architectural drawings, some writings, and manuscript illuminations which, in the course of illustrating the building of the Temple of Solomon or the Tower of Babel, show us many useful details of builders at work. Architectural drawings survive in surprising numbers, while in a slightly different category are the instruction manuals published in Germany in the very late fifteenth century and the sixteenth, which purport to explain how to draw up certain designs. What hardly survives at all, however, is any account of how building was done.

There are three very famous medieval documents — the mid-twelfth-century account by Abbot Suger of Saint-Denis of the building and decoration of the new choir of his abbey church, the account written c. 1200 by Gervase, monk of Canterbury, of the *Burning and repair of Canterbury Cathedral*, and the thirteenth-century *Portfolio* of Villard de Honnecourt, consisting of a set of drawings, plans and designs including buildings, mouldings and building machinery — all of which have been cited many times as sources for medieval building practices. Of the three, Suger's account tells us much about the man himself and the decoration of his church, but little about the building, although he does, inadvertently and in passing, drop some valuable hints about it. Detailed study of Villard's *Portfolio* has thrown severe doubt on his claims to have built churches, and indeed on his understanding of architecture, while his drawings, although interesting, are no longer generally thought to be those either of an architect or of a masons' workshop.

Gervase's text, on the other hand, is the only surviving medieval description of a team of masons at work, and it gives much information both about masonic practice and about some building processes.

The real evidence of how masons worked lies in the buildings themselves and in surviving building accounts. These are the fabric rolls and account books that record day-to-day expenditure on building materials and wages. From the lists of purchases and occasional references to a part of the building it can be possible to work out the building history. They also give, indirectly, a lot of information about the numbers of workmen, what they did and the order in which they did it. The most complete set of such accounts is undoubtedly that of the English royal office of works, which is continuous from the reign of Henry III (1215-72). As the king was the most active builder in the country, the royal building accounts concern an enormous number and variety of buildings. Two recently published sets of non-royal fabric rolls have, however, vastly increased our understanding of medieval building processes: these are the building accounts from the cathedrals of Exeter and Troyes, and many examples will be taken from them for this book.

These records are primarily administrative, rarely explicit, and take no account of the demands of architectural historians. Their immense variety is, however, informative in itself. Medieval life was rarely systematic, and the building records clearly demonstrate the adaptability of the administrative machine as it found new solutions as problems arose. A great medieval building was a complex achievement in administration, design and engineering. Without a pragmatic and flexible approach to all these aspects, no buildings would have been erected at all; this flexible pragmatism can be clearly detected at every level of the enterprise.

6 *Opposite* Fifteenth-century miniature in the *Bedford Hours* showing the building of the Tower of Babel (see Genesis, xi, 1-9). Manuscript illuminations are a good source of information about medieval building methods: this picture shows activities such as mixing mortar, measuring and cutting stone, hoisting stones, and, at the top, a mason falling from the scaffolding while his colleagues look on.

7 The nave of Exeter Cathedral, built *c*. 1328-42. Progress was recorded in the 'Fabric Rolls', the building accounts, which survive fully enough for the reconstruction of the entire Cathedral to be established exactly.

THE MASONS' LODGE

THE LODGE

Every building project was based upon the masons' lodge. In its literal sense this was the hut attached to the building site where the masons did their indoor work, stored their tools and ate their lunch. The term does, however, have a wider meaning: the late medieval lodges attached to the apparently endless campaigns on big south German cathedrals such as Ulm, Strasbourg and Cologne had a sufficient degree of permanence to become in a sense institutional, and when a group of representatives from these lodges came together in 1459 to draw up the set of regulations known as the Regensburg Ordinances, they seemed to see the lodge (*Bauhütte*) as an organisation capable of controlling training, employment and the administration of the works. The lodge is often referred to by modern writers in this broader sense, but while it clearly contains a kernel of truth for late medieval Germany, the evidence for other regions and at earlier times is more tenuous. These late medieval regulations and ordinances contain the earliest formal references to training or a lodge structure,

The king and his master mason, from Matthew Paris' *Life of SS Alban and Amphibalus*. The master mason carries his compasses and set square, and is showing the king round the building site. Patrons such as King Henry III of England, during whose reign the book was written, took a close interest in their buildings and were on good terms with their architects.

8 *Opposite* The masons' lodge, shown in this fifteenth-century miniature as an open-sided, thatched building next to the site. It was used to store tools, to protect the cutting masons from the weather, and as a place to sit and eat lunch.

and while such a structure may well have existed, other sources give the impression of a far less formal kind of organisation.

The lodge in this second sense is, however, stressed by modern scholars, partly owing to the lingering influence of Freemasonry and partly because masons were outside the normal medieval craft structure. Medieval crafts, especially those based in cities, developed trade guilds that regulated work and conditions, and through which apprentices could be indentured; but masons, both owing to the peripatetic nature of their work and because patronage was largely dispensed by great individuals or independent institutions, could not participate in this guild system. Only from the late thirteenth century is there any evidence of indentured apprenticeship. When it did occur it lasted between five and seven years; the master was allowed one apprentice at a time and was paid a fee, while the apprentice

received a wage. The earliest masons' guilds date from the fourteenth century in large cities such as London, where the municipality evidently wanted to exert some control over their activities. It was only in Italy and the German Empire that the city authorities controlled important building enterprises and the masons who worked on them. By the sixteenth century in Germany the control of building in cities was formally organised. For example, Hans Beheim was appointed city architect to Nuremberg in 1503, responsible for the design, planning and construction of buildings in the city, but his activities were to be supervised by the municipal architect, who was a member of the town council. In countries such as England and France the patrons were the Church, the king and greater magnates, and the relationship between the patron and the master mason, which could personally be close, was focused on the site. The lodge, providing shelter and security,

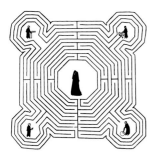

11 The labyrinth of Reims Cathedral recorded before its destruction. The Cathedral architects were so valued that they were depicted in the corners.

would inevitably become the centre of such organisation as there was.

The Regensburg Ordinances indicate that in mid-fifteenth-century Germany, at least, some sort of training path was thought to be desirable. Why masons from the big German lodges felt that they had to draw up regulations at all is far from clear, but they may have wished to control entry to the profession and correct abuse. The Regensburg meeting authorised lodges such as Cologne and Ulm to run the *Hüttenfürdrung*, the system of advancement within the lodge from apprentice through journeyman to master. A journeyman who had successfully completed the *Fürdrung* would possess the skills necessary to practise his craft. According to the Ordinances this involved above all the ability to take an elevation from a

ground-plan, which effectively meant knowing how to draw up the building design. Medieval illustrations of master masons invariably identify them by their main drawing instruments, the set square and dividers or compasses, and it was as designers and supervisors that they were seen by their contemporaries. Gervase noted William of Sens delivering 'moulds' to his men, and a famous sermon by a thirteenth-century Dominican, Nicholas de Biard, remarks: 'The master masons, with rod and glove in hand, say to the others, "Cut it for me here"...'. The labyrinth set into the floor of Reims Cathedral featured Jean d'Orbais setting out the plan of the chevet. The much-discussed 'secret' of the medieval mason is likely to have been knowledge of the geometrical methods used to make the draw-

generations, show what must have been a common pattern, which seems far removed from the formalities of Regensburg. Adam Vertue was a competent professional mason whose sons, Robert and William, rose to great eminence; the third generation in the person of Robert junior, while producing beautiful work, declined once more into the status of competent professional. Adam and Robert senior are recorded at Westminster Abbey in 1475, Robert clearly still a novice, being paid at half his father's wage. Adam, who died ten years later, was proficient enough to be entrusted to make fireplaces for some new rooms at Eltham Palace, but we hear no more of him. Robert had become a Master Mason to the King by 1499 at the latest, and before his death in 1506 he had designed Henry VII's chapel in Westminster Abbey and, with his brother William, had begun Bath Abbey church; he had also probably worked at St George's Chapel, Windsor Castle. Of Bath, Robert and William asserted that, 'Of the vawte devised for the chancelle there shall be noone so goodly neither in England nor in France. And thereof they make theym fast and sure.'

William Vertue, who lived until 1527, was able to develop his career more fully. Besides finishing the works he had started with Robert, he was King's Master Mason at the Tower of London, continued to work at Windsor, and was also involved with buildings at Eton, Oxford and Cambridge. At Oxford he designed Corpus Christi College, and at Cambridge he seems to have exploited the experience gained from building the fan vaults of Bath Abbey by acting as consultant for those of King's College chapel.

Robert's son, Robert junior, was quite young when his father died but he was not, it seems, taken on as an apprentice by his uncle William. Robert junior attained the position of master mason to Evesham Abbey, which, while respectable enough, did not match the achievements of the earlier generation. In all the records of the Vertues and countless others, on the Continent as well as in Britain, there is no hint of the kind of lodge organisation described in the Regensburg Ordinances. Rather, the

10 *Opposite, top* The master mason's main task was to design the building and all its details. This was well understood by contemporaries, who always identified him by his drawing instruments. This early fourteenth-century manuscript shows him with his compasses and set square, with which he could design mouldings and tracery and establish proportions.

12 *Above* Thirteenth-century miniature showing the master mason supervising stone cutting.

ings, knowledge that would certainly have set masons apart from other workers, but, again, the talk of 'secrets' does not occur before the fifteenth century, and the information would in practice have been impossible to keep secret. The important point is that the Ordinances presume that the geometry was taught by master to pupil in the lodge as an essential element in the lodge tradition.

The notion of the lodge as given in the late medieval Ordinances (and taken over by the Brotherhood of Freemasons) is not incompatible with the evidence of a looser masonic structure that emerges from other sources, but these latter do nevertheless give a different impression. The Vertue family in late medieval England, who can be traced through three

13 *Opposite* The fan vaults over the choir of Bath Abbey designed by Robert and William Vertue in the early sixteenth century, and which they alleged would be better than any in England or France.

14 *Right* The tomb slab of Hugues Libergier, architect of St Nicaise, Reims. Hugues died in 1263, at the time when the master mason was becoming a recognised figure in society. His tomb slab, now in Reims Cathedral, shows him clasping a model of St Nicaise, holding his staff, and surrounded by his drawing instruments.

Gmünd by his father, Heinrich, and in Prague he trained his own sons, Wenzel, Johann and Janco. A significant number of masons have names associated with the big quarries; the building site and the quarry were closely associated, with masons working at either, and it is likely that basic cutting skills were learned in the quarry. The more delicate skills, however, were taught in the lodge. By the time a young mason became a journeyman he would have to know how to cut intricate shapes for keystones, voussoirs, vault, capital and base mouldings, and he may also by that stage have had some knowledge of drawing up designs.

Once trained, the journeyman apparently practised his craft for several years at different building sites, often far from home. Masons did not move about in coherent groups, although there is occasional evidence of loyalty to a particular master, as at Troyes in 1392-3, when Henry de Bruisselles left the cathedral site, taking with him *les ouvriers de la loge*. This period in a mason's life has been designated by German scholars the *Wanderjahr* or wandering year, and its existence goes largely unquestioned, although evidence is at best circumstantial. Masons were undoubtedly mobile, and the stylistic affinities of buildings show influences from impressive distances, but how far the wandering years were formally constituted seems debatable; rather, they would appear to have been an inevitable and natural process. It is certain, however, that a journeyman could not become a master without several years of building experience.

THE MASTER MASON

Although no building could be realised without the co-operation of the patron and the building administrators, the pivotal being in the whole enterprise was the master mason. Some indication of his role is already apparent in the monk Gervase's account of William of Sens, master mason of the new choir of Canterbury Cathedral: 'He addressed himself to the procuring of stone beyond the sea. He constructed ingenious machines for loading and unloading ships, and for drawing cement and stones. He delivered moulds [templates] for

evidence is of early independence following a period learning on the site.

Most masons seem to have been trained on the site. In 1359 John of Evesham contracted with the Dean and chapter of Hereford Cathedral to become master mason for life on condition that he instructed the workforce in techniques of masonry and carpentry. Where the craft ran in families sons could be trained by their fathers: Peter Parler, the architect of Prague Cathedral, was almost certainly trained in the south German town of Schwäbisch-

15 Peter Parler, the architect of Prague Cathedral and the greatest in a dynasty of fine architects. This self-portrait bust, placed high in the choir of the Cathedral in about 1390, is one of a series depicting its imperial founders and high ecclesiastics, and shows that the master mason was now considered worthy of inclusion in their number.

shaping the stones to the sculptors who were assembled, and diligently prepared other things of the same kind.' Contractor, designer and engineer, the master mason's presence was theoretically required at every stage of the building process, and as buildings became more complicated and demand grew for competent master masons, so their status and power increased. In their own sphere they were answerable to no-one, as the late medieval regulations indicate when they require a mason new to a building site to satisfy the master mason (not the administrators) of his competence.

Master masons inevitably left more traces in the records than their subordinates. Their consciousness of themselves as estimable in-

dividuals surfaces in the thirteenth century, when they were buried inside churches in handsome tombs, such as that of Hugues Lib- 14 ergier, the architect of St Nicaise at Reims, who was buried there in 1263. His inscribed slab depicts him in a long robe carrying the tools of his trade. At about the same time an inscription was placed in the south transept of Notre-Dame, Paris, recording the date of the foundation and the name of the architect Jean de Chelles, while Pierre de Montreuil, the mid-thirteenth-century master mason of Saint-Germain-des-Prés Abbey in Paris, was so distinguished a figure that his tombstone described him as *doctor lathomorum* and his wife was allowed to share his tomb inside the church. Just over a century later Peter Parler could carve his self-portrait high in the choir of Prague Cathedral along with the busts of the 15 Holy Roman Emperor and leading churchmen.

The Parler self-portrait reveals the esteem held by a patron for his architect, the signs of which are again first detectable in the thirteenth century. The lost labyrinths set in the floors of Amiens and Reims Cathedrals as penance paths for pilgrims recorded the names of the cathedral architects and the founding bishops. These were placed in the church by the clergy, and the attitude they betray is in marked contrast to that of Abbot Suger of Saint-Denis who, writing in the 1140s, failed to mention his architects at all. In the late Middle Ages a patron could take the master mason into his household, where he would rank with the esquires, eating at their table and receiving, like one Master Geoffrey at St Albans in 1314, 'a robe yearly of the suit of the abbot's squires.' Guy Dammartin, architect to the Duke of Berry, was listed for payment purposes in the Duke's household, and Raymond du Temple, who worked for the Duke's brother, Charles v of France, was a serjeant-at-arms. This equation with rank possibly helped the household clerks to establish the correct pay and status for a figure who did not fit into normal household structures, but Raymond was also an advisor to the king; and James of St George, architect of Edward I's castles in Wales, became Constable of Harlech for three years, no doubt living in the comfortable rooms that he had himself designed.

A master mason's reputation could be high enough for him to be summoned considerable distances: Mathias of Arras, predecessor to Peter Parler at Prague, was called from Narbonne in the south of France. A Frenchman, Etienne de Bonneuil, was summoned to Uppsala in Sweden; and in the late fourteenth century successive German and French masters were invited to Italy to advise the cathedral authorities at Milan. Their fame naturally also spread among themselves, and in at least one instance became the stuff of myth: the influence of the Parler workshop in Prague, which sent many trained masons to building sites all over Germany, lingered through to the end of the fifteenth century, when the *Junker von Prag* (young men of Prague) were hailed by the writers of instruction manuals as their mentors.

In the later Middle Ages master masons diversified into such activities as quarry ownership and contracting to supply stone; when undertaking a job, they increasingly contracted to supply either materials or labour or both. Although early on masons tended to do work at task, contracting for a specific small job such as building a wall, contracting for a major building enterprise had become quite usual by the end of the Middle Ages, when a successful mason-contractor such as Henry Yeveley could run a business supplying materials even where he was not the master mason. William Orchard of Oxford also did this, selling stone from his leased quarry at Headington. Such arrangements give insights into masons' accumulated wealth, as they required considerable initial capital, which was evidently not always forthcoming: at Châteaudun in 1272 one Gilotin contracted to build a grange giving his own possessions as guarantee. Late medieval Spanish contracts, such as that drawn up in 1451 between Guillermo Vilosolar and the authorities of Salamanca Cathedral, specified that the master mason provide plant, tools, materials and labour. Employers, then as now, sought value for money: in 1381 Jean Besançon won the contract to build a spiral staircase in the ducal palace at Bourges because he tendered 35 sous per stair against the 40 demanded by Jean Corbeilly.

Activities such as quarry ownership, contracting and property dealing could make a lot of money, but took up time. In addition, a successful master with a flourishing practice could be in charge of several buildings at once and would need to divide his time between them: Ulrich von Ensingen was master mason at both Strasbourg and Ulm; and Hans von Burghausen, master mason of St Martin at Landshut in Bavaria, was building several other churches at the same time. The master was, however, obliged to supervise the construction, and the anxiety of the authorities on this point is reflected in many contracts. These might stipulate that a master must not leave the site during the course of the work, or they might contain penalty clauses, such as the 1368 contract of Robert de Patrington, which specified that if he was working elsewhere and failed to return to York at the third time of asking, his salary would cease until he reappeared. Some practical way out of the difficulty was sometimes found: Eudes de Montreuil was allowed to keep two horses at the Palais in Paris, and Arnolfo di Cambio was given horses when he held posts concurrently at Rome and Perugia. On several occasions in 1511 the desperate authorities at Troyes Cathedral despatched messengers to Beauvais with spare horses to fetch Martin Chambiges, who was refusing to attend to his duties at Troyes.

The problem was overcome by the appointment of deputies, the earliest recorded instance of which is at Canterbury after William of Sens fell from the scaffolding and from his bed supervised for a short time 'a certain ingenious monk' (in the coy words of Gervase) who directed operations on the site. Later, however, the role was formalised in the person of a Warden or overseer, who acted as technical supervisor in the master's absence, and sometimes succeeded as master, as at Strasbourg where Ulrich von Ensingen's position was taken by his warden, Johann Hultz. The warden was a fully qualified master in his own right: Arnold von Westfalen, a leading master mason of fifteenth-century Germany, who pioneered the beautiful form of vaulting known as the cell vault, worked as a master in the 1450s, returned in the next decade to act as warden to his former master, and in the 1470s became master mason to the court at Meissen. The warden was also responsible for many of the design details, so that at, for instance, Edward I's castles in Wales it can be difficult to distinguish the work of the master mason, James of St George, from that of his deputy, Walter of Hereford, and it seems likely that James set out the plan and Walter supervised the construction, designing such details as door mouldings himself.

THE WORKING DAY

The ordinary lodge that was needed on every site was impermanent, created for a building campaign and dismantled when it was over. The lodge was built as soon as work started; its provision was the responsibility of the master mason, as is shown by a payment in 1448 to Elizabeth Janyns, wife of the master mason of Merton College, Oxford, for four days' work bringing straw to thatch the lodge. Manuscript illuminations show the lodge as an open-sided wooden hut next to the building, but the cutaway effect is probably a device to help the artist show what is going on inside. Large, permanent sites had durable buildings, often with more than one room, although few were as large as the 50m x 14m lodge built at Poitiers in 1385. The lodge had in practice to be large enough for every skilled mason to have a place at the banker where the more intricately moulded stones were cut. Attached to it, or conveniently near, were the tracing house, where the designs were drawn, and the forge, where the tools were sharpened. If the lodge were not secure the tools were kept elsewhere: in fifteenth-century Segovia (Spain) the storage room was at the base of the cathedral tower, and was to be converted to a safe store when the masons left.

No-one lived in the lodge. The master mason either owned a house or rented one from the patron (or was given one). In a short building campaign he was responsible for housing the workforce, but large establishments provided hostels or lodgings, as at Exeter, where the masons lived at the edge of the precinct near the tracing house and carpenter's store. At Strasbourg they had a house with a paid cook, and an inventory of 1406-7 from the Basle house records thirteen beds, bed- and table-linen, washstands, cooking pots and tableware, all looked after by a housekeeper. The men bought their own food except on feastdays. There was no universal rule about this, but if food was supplied wages were usually lower. In 1337 the masons of Siena won a thirty-year fight to be given wine from the cathedral vineyards, on the grounds that they wasted too much time queueing in the city taverns. The masons were, however, regularly given their workclothes: at Westminster they received hoods, gloves, boots for wet weather, straw hats for the summer and a robe (a furred one for the master).

In theory, building was a seasonal activity, ceasing from Michaelmas (29 September) until Easter, and in practice from All Saints (1 November) until the Purification of the Virgin (2 February). Work was confined during these winter months to designing and cutting stone. Working hours were fairly similar across Europe, effectively lasting from sunrise to sunset, with time off for breakfast, lunch (and a siesta in summer) and a drink. The Germans, then as now, worked slightly longer hours than the English. Hours were much longer in summer than on short winter days, although there are occasional instances, in royal building works such as Eton College, of the men working on by candlelight. The earliest surviving regulations, which attempt to lay down working conditions, are from York in 1352, but they reflect earlier practice and demonstrate that on an ecclesiastical site the masons were obliged to conform to the requirements of the liturgical hours. On Saturdays and feastdays worked stopped at 'none', which by the late Middle Ages had ceased to represent the monastic hour of None (the ninth hour, i.e. three o'clock pm) and was closer to midday (i.e. noon). In Freiburg, however, Saturday work continued until five o'clock, but every fourteen days work finished at three o'clock so that the masons could go to the baths.

The master mason worked to a contract of employment, usually earning about twice as much as a journeyman, with additional perquisites. Journeymen were either paid at task for a specific job, or received a daily wage, usually paid weekly, with less in winter and no pay for feastdays, of which there were a great many. It is impossible to quantify pay in modern terms, and individuals were paid according to their skills. There were many categories of mason, broadly divided into roughmasons (unskilled) and freemasons (skilled), and a large project such as Westminster Abbey would employ hewers, layers, wallers, marblers, image-makers and paviors, each at a different rate of pay. In England a journeyman earned about 4 pence a day before the Black Death (1349-51) and about 6 pence after it, when there was a shortage of skilled labour. In England, too, a master was paid whether he worked a particular day or not, but in France and elsewhere a fairly standard agreement was that made in 1286 between Jean Deschamps and the cathedral works at Narbonne: 3 sous for each day that he was present, an annual robe and 100 sous per year towards the maintenance of the house that he rented from the chapter. There could be variations on this, a particularly striking one being the contract secured by one Martin Lonay in 1264, who was paid 2 sous per day worked if he arrived on the site before noon, with 100 sous per annum on top. He was also to be given food for himself and his horse. In 1129 Raymondo, master at Lugo in Spain, arranged that in the event of a fall in the value of money he should be paid in kind, with silver, linen, wood, shoes, meat, salt and candles. Jaime Fabre, who lived in Palma di Mallorca, was paid travelling expenses while he was master mason at Barcelona. At other times and other places, however, conditions were more austere: great masters such as Peter Parler of Prague and Conrad Roriczer of Regensburg were paid solely for the days that they worked, although at Regensburg both master and men were given extra when the cathedral was roofed or (in modern terms)

'topped out'. In Italy, where major building works were the responsibility of the commune, the city would exempt the *capomaestro* from income tax; and in 1257 John of Gloucester, master mason to Henry III of England, was exempted not only from some taxes but also from jury service, as later was the mason-contractor Henry Yeveley.

The masons' agreements reflect their preoccupation with sickness and old age. Journeymen had little security. As insurance against emergency the Strasbourg lodge put aside 1 pfennig a week for each worker, but a mason could not necessarily expect help after an accident — although Louis IX of France gave sick pay to a mason who broke his leg at Royaumont Abbey in 1234. A master who was unable to supervise the work could not do his job, and once it was seen that William of Sens would not recover sufficiently from his accident at Canterbury in 1178 he was forced to return to France. It is not surprising, therefore, to find careful pension arrangements. At Urgel in Spain Raymond the Lombard was to receive a pension equivalent to that of a cathedral canon. Spanish terms seem always to have been generous: in fourteenth-century England, John Bell of Durham would, in the event of great age or infirmity, receive a pension of 4 marks. English contracts, however, often take account of illness. In 1351 William de Hoton agreed with the chapter of York that if he became blind or incurably ill, half his salary would go to pay a deputy; and in 1368 Robert de Patrington, a successor to William, contracted to receive a pension if he was prevented from working through blindness or infirmity, so long as he continued to give advice. This seems less harsh than the fate of William of Sens two centuries earlier, but the interesting point is that these English contracts imply a sense on the employer's part of obligation to the master for life.

THE BUILDING

ADMINISTRATION

The sheer scale of a great medieval building operation necessitated careful and continuous administration, in raising and spending money and in organising the building works and the labour force. The different types of patron, private and institutional, and the varying arrangements they made with their master masons, make it impossible to generalise about the organisation of the administration. In any case, much depended on the purpose of the building project.

A castle, for instance, would for military reasons normally need to be built very quickly, and it would require huge sums of money and an enormous labour force. A church, however, frequently became the victim of indifference on the patron's part once the choir, the liturgically important area, was built, and work could be delayed for years. The cathedrals of Beauvais and Cologne are two famous examples of this situation: the former was never finished and the latter was completed only in the nineteenth century. Expenditure at Edward I's eight new castles in Wales was truly awesome, as were the numbers of workmen employed. Nearly £6000, a huge sum then, was spent in one season at Conwy, and Harlech, which was built mostly in one seven-year campaign, cost over £8000. Between 1277 and 1339 the total expenditure on the castles amounted to £93,000. It had been the habit of the royal works to impress labour from all over England, county by county, but in 1282 labour was impressed on a wholly new scale: 1000 diggers, 345 carpenters and 50 masons gathered at Chester and Bristol, and were sent into Wales to start preliminary work on the castle sites; and one July week at contents page Harlech in 1286, 227 masons were employed, with a supporting cast of 115 quarriers, 30 smiths, 22 carpenters and 546 general workmen. It is perhaps salutary to observe that the total number of clerks required to administer this force of nearly 1000 men was four.

A cathedral works rarely if ever occupied a labour force of this size, but it often lasted for many years, and a small group would be permanently required for maintenance. A report on the fabric at York in 1344 stated that the masons had so little to do that they were quarrelling. The main building campaign on Chartres Cathedral lasted about forty years; the choir of Canterbury Cathedral was built in only ten years, with a one-year break when funds ran out, but the glazing programme lasted for another thirty years. The Gothic work at Exeter Cathedral, which amounted to an almost total rebuilding, took more than seventy years to complete.

In a large secular organisation such as the royal works the administration was run by the clerk of the works: among the fourteenth-century holders of that office were William of Wykeham — who later, as Bishop of Winchester, became a great patron in his own right — and the poet Geoffrey Chaucer. The administration of a monastic building works was normally run by a monastic official, the sacrist. A cathedral works was run by the *Custos fabricae* or *magister operis*, chosen from among the canons. In northern Europe the cathedral was independent of the city authorities and money was more often than not provided by the bishop, although administered by chapter officials. At Strasbourg, however, by 1205 the cathedral fabric was administered by the city magistracy through an organisation known as the Oeuvre Notre-Dame, for which a special administrative headquarters was built in 1274 (its sixteenth-century successor is the cathedral museum). In Italy cathedral works were also usually run by the city authorities, with responsibility for day-to-day administration delegated to a clerk of the works; in Germany, too, masons would be employed by the city.

The existence of an established administration guaranteed architectural continuity. This was important: Beauvais Cathedral and Westminster Abbey are two of many buildings that show the efforts of later architects to harmonise their ideas with earlier parts of the building. The Regensburg Ordinances even forbid an incoming master mason to change his predecessor's design. The works also relieved the master mason of some responsibility: unless the master supplied materials and labour the clerk of the works bought supplies and paid the wages, enabling the master mason to concentrate on the technical side, although in the English royal works he was often forced to make up a weekly account sheet.

A building operation needed a continuous supply of money for materials and wages, and if it were not forthcoming the work stopped, as can be illustrated by the building history of St Stephen's Chapel in the Palace of Westminster, where the three widely separated building campaigns, beginning in 1292, exactly reflected the financial situation of Edward I and his two successors as king. The later stages of a building could be even more costly, as the shapes of the stones for parts such as vaulting were more complex and therefore more expensive to carve, and they had to be lifted further with more elaborate equipment. Money was raised much as it is now, by taxes, gifts and appeals. The will of Thomas Sampson, canon of York, drawn up in 1346, leaves £20 to the fabric of the proposed new choir of the Minster, provided it be started within a year, 'as I have repeatedly said to Master Thomas Ludham [clerk to the fabric] and Thomas Pacenham [master mason]', a clause that gives a charming vignette of the three officials in close discussion of a matter dear to all their hearts. Royal building projects were often financed by heavy borrowing or by the diversion of funds from specific estates; the chapter of Beauvais did the same in 1225 when it diverted the revenues of all vacant benefices in the diocese for ten years. In 1342 King John of Bohemia took a cut from the profits of the silver mines at Kutna Hora to finance the proposed new cathedral in Prague. Magnates could give timber or rights in quarries. In 1292 the citizens of Orvieto had to pay a building tax, but when this was tried in France, where the town was independent of the cathedral, the townspeople rioted if the tax

became too high (riots prevented building for several seasons during the 1230s at Reims and Beauvais). There money had to be raised from the rural tenantry, and Chartres Cathedral, for example, owes its existence to the prosperous arable land that surrounds the city.

The faithful could be cajoled through appeals and indulgences, the most celebrated instance of the latter being the permission granted to the citizens of Rouen to eat butter during Lent in exchange for the money that largely financed the Tour de Beurre on the cathedral façade. Appeals played not on feelings of guilt but on the desire for salvation, with relic processions through the diocese (a thirteenth-century abbot of St Albans was particularly successful at this) and offerings of the faithful, especially at shrines, which could themselves be exploited when the time came to rebuild. The monks of Durham, for example, stressed the need for a suitable setting for the shrine of St Cuthbert when the choir vault collapsed in the thirteenth century; and when the choir of St Albans needed rebuilding in 1257 the grave of St Alban was miraculously discovered near the high altar. The phenomenon in twelfth-century France known as the Cult of Carts, when the people, in a state of high nervous excitement, helped to drag the carts of stone to the building site, was, however, an event in which pious hysteria was carefully directed by a few churchmen acting in concert; it had no future and was atypical.

Surviving building accounts are rare, but the evidence tends the same way across Europe, showing increased attention to detail and the abandonment of Latin for the native language as the need became stronger for precision in technical terms (although the meaning of many medieval building terms eludes us still). An account book survives from early fourteenth-century Westminster, but most English accounts of that date are on rolls of parchment membranes, about 20 cm (8 inches) wide and sewn in a continuous strip. The accounts (the fabric rolls) were kept in four-yearly terms, drawn up weekly, with receipts and expenditure separated, wages and materials differentiated and specified. By the late

16 The Butter Tower, the south tower on the west façade of Rouen Cathedral, was financed by Indulgences (days off Purgatory) granted to people who paid for permission to eat butter during Lent but who gave the money to the building works.

17 *Opposite* The patron is shown round the site by the master mason, who has evidently ensured that the masons will be working hard during the visit; they are using axes and chisels, and the master mason can test with the square he carries the right angles produced.

fourteenth century in Troyes they were kept in books and written on paper, as in fifteenth-century Germany. Accounting there was half-yearly, at Strasbourg in December (the feast of St Lucy) and June (SS Vitus and Modestus). By the fifteenth century only Prague and Basle were still keeping accounts in Latin.

Relations between the patron and the builders were close, and not only at the financial level. There are many illustrations of the patron being shown the site by the master mason, and although royalty are recorded indulging in such empty gestures as Louis IX carrying stone in the Holy Land or Edward I wheeling a barrow, written sources confirm that the patrons' actions were not always symbolic but could actually help in practical ways. Abbot Suger of Saint-Denis left a perhaps unwittingly vivid account of himself harrying the workforce and leading expeditions to find suitable timber; and Bishop Stapeldon of Exeter bought painting materials in London for the Exeter works. Designs of both churches and castles can be seen changing to meet new liturgical or military demands, and the request for change came from the patrons even if the final design was the work of the architect. It is generally presumed that Edward I worked closely with his castle designer, James of St George, whom he brought from Savoy. In the late fourteenth century the French royal family actually shared architects: the new work at the Louvre was entrusted by Charles V to Raymond du Temple, among whose assistants were Guy and Drouet de Dammartin. Guy and Drouet subsequently went to work for Charles' brothers, the Dukes of Berry and Burgundy, and when Guy died Drouet came from Dijon to Bourges as master mason. As clerk of the works under Edward III, William of Wykeham had met William Wynford, whom he later employed to design his colleges at Winchester and Oxford. Sometimes, however, relations went wrong: Hans Niesenberger, a fifteenth-century mason working in Germany, managed at various times to quarrel with both his patrons and the workforce, and in about 1200 St Albans Abbey suffered from the 'deceitful and unreliable' behaviour of the master mason Hugh de

Goldclif, who gave bad advice, recommending expensive additions which he then allowed to fall into ruin. It is perhaps not surprising that those in charge of a terrifyingly large budget should take a close interest in the building. How far the patrons actively assisted in the design process is, however, another matter.

DESIGN

All the evidence indicates that although the building design was drawn up by the master mason in collaboration with the patron, the intervention of the latter was at a strictly non-technical level. Abbot Suger's lack of interest in the technical details of the remarkable building created for him at Saint-Denis is notorious. Alan of Walsingham, the sacrist in charge of the new work at Ely in the 1320s, is still credited with the design of the great octagonal crossing, but even if the idea was his (there is no contemporary evidence), the structure itself was set out by a master referred to in the records as 'someone from London'. The patron could impose his own taste on the design details: Henry VI specified that the chapel at King's College, Cambridge, should be built 'in large forme, clene and substancial, settynge a parte superfluite of too gret curious werkes of entail and besy moulding'. Deference to the patron's wishes is shown in the contract of 1398 between John Bell and Durham Cathedral priory, which states that the prior shall choose the design of the great window in the south gable of the new dormitory. Some years earlier, however, William de Helpeston had secured the right at Vale Royal Abbey to 'change and ordain his templates as he wished . . . without challenge from anyone'. The quality of work at Durham was to be based on that of Brancepeth Castle, and design as well as quality control was often decided by reference to other buildings, as in Henry III's famous request for the vault of St George's Chapel, Windsor, to be like that of Lichfield Cathedral. Much was transmitted by the collective visual memory of an age in which images were for many a more significant form of communication than writing.

We have already noted that, to his contem-

18 The south gable of the new dormitory of Durham Cathedral priory, completed in 1398. The surviving contract states that the prior shall choose the design of the window tracery.

poraries, the master mason was seen as the designer, almost always identified by his drawing instruments. He (or sometimes his deputy) was responsible for all the details, and some scholars are confident that they can use moulding profiles to attribute a building to an individual master or workshop, although the very different designs known to have been drawn up by the thirteenth-century French mason Gautier de Varinfoy make even this uncertain. Even when the general disposition of a building was designed to harmonise with earlier parts, the moulding profiles were designed in an up-to-date style. Designs spread quickly, however, either because a master would repeat, say, a tracery pattern at another building, or because he copied ideas from elsewhere. In the thirteenth century Villard de Honnecourt was sketching buildings that interested him, down to quite small details; while he may not have been a working mason, there is evidence by the late fourteenth century if not earlier that patrons were sending their masons on study visits. In 1393 Philip, Duke of Burgundy sent his sculptor Claus Sluter to look at Mehun-sur-Yèvre, the château being built by his brother the Duke of Berry, and in 1412/13 Mehun and Bourges attracted the notice of the Troyes Cathedral authorities, who sent Jehan de Nantes to sketch the towers as possible models for the proposed towers at Troyes. Despite the efforts of the German lodges of the fifteenth century to keep designs to themselves, there was in practice no such thing as copyright: the sets of beautiful chancel fittings in the parish churches of Heckington in Lincolnshire and Hawton in Nottinghamshire show that a similar programme could be carried out at two places by different groups of masons within a very few years of each other. The late thirteenth-century work at York Minster perhaps shows us the different contributions of patron and architect: the general design of the nave elevation is strikingly French, but the mouldings are in local taste, which may indicate that the patron, who had spent some time in Paris, asked for a French design, which was drawn up and executed by the master mason and his team. That the master mason himself knew

19 Mehun-sur-Yèvre, the château built near Bourges, by the Duke of Berry in the late fourteenth century, and here depicted in the *Très Riches Heures,* painted for the Duke by the Limbourg brothers. So famous was the building that Berry's brother, the Duke of Burgundy, sent his own sculptors from Dijon to study it.

20 *Left* Later additions to buildings, as shown here in the eastern bays of the nave of Beverley Minster, were often made to look like the earlier parts, with only details such as mouldings and window tracery brought up to date. At the extreme right, the thirteenth-century capitals are plain except for the use of Purbeck marble. All the other capitals, dating from the fourteenth century, have foliage additions, and Purbeck marble has been abandoned. The mouldings and pier forms are otherwise identical to the earlier work.

21 *Right* The nave of York Minster, begun in 1291. It has a strikingly French style of elevation, stressing flatness and verticality, probably because its patron, Archbishop John le Romeyn, had spent several years in Paris.

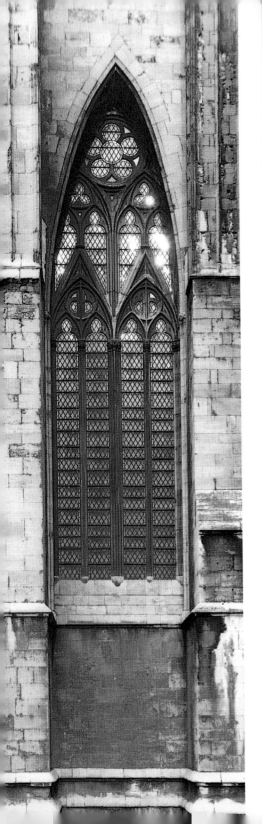

22 and **23** A window in the vestibule of York chapter house (far left) displaying a curious design of a gable and cut quatrefoil, which otherwise appears only at St Urbain in Troyes (left). This kind of detail would have been sketched by a master mason on his travels and employed on his return home.

various buildings in France is, however, suggested by an idiosyncratic tracery pattern in the chapter house vestibule, which was almost [22] certainly borrowed from St Urbain in Troyes, [23] and is the kind of small, fiddly detail that would be picked up by a mason rather than a patron. Except for Villard's sketches and drawings, however, nothing survives that can be described as a copy of an existing building.

A large number of medieval architectural drawings and sketches survives. In the late Middle Ages the big German lodges, such as Ulm, Strasbourg and Vienna, built up collections of drawings, and some scholars speak of a Viennese lodge drawing style. Scarce from before the thirteenth century, architectural drawings become numerous from the fourteenth, when complex designs of mouldings, vault patterns and tracery made them more desirable, and the gradual substitution of paper for parchment made them cheaper to produce. The very durability of parchment contributed to the disappearance of drawings, as it can be palimpsested (scraped down and reused); one of the earliest thirteenth-century drawings, of a north French church façade, has been palimpsested and the parchment made into a church book.

These drawings comprise vault patterns, façades, ground-plans and plans of piers, tracery and ornamental details. Before the sixteenth century they were neither scaled nor annotated, and they are clearly several steps away from a working drawing. Ironically enough, the only ones that even hint at three-dimensionality are in the *Portfolio* of Villard, who was probably not an architect; otherwise they are orthogonal projections in two dimen- [24] sions, with no indication of depth, and some show several levels of the buildings superimposed. Two early fourteenth-century drawings for the façade of Orvieto Cathedral may be competition pieces, as they are by different hands and one is closer to the finished building than the other. Some are variations on well-known buildings, others designs that were never apparently realised. They can be [25] enormous (the façade plan F for Cologne Cathedral is 4 m x 1.70 m, drawn on eleven

membranes sewn together, and the façade [27] drawing for Strasbourg, made *c*.1360, is 4 m high). They are often beautifully finished in black ink with details shaded in colour.

These drawings are studio work. The architect was exploring possibilities, or preparing a drawing to show to the client, a practice attested in the records, although the specification was itself often set out verbally in great detail. The windows to be made at Salamanca by Guillermo Vilosolar were to be 'according to the design that I have delivered to you', and a contract of 1373 at Boxley Abbey, Kent, states that the mouldings and tracery should be made according to the agreed designs. In 1381 alternative designs were drawn up for the new choir screen at Troyes Cathedral so that the chapter could choose between them.

The Troyes records, however, give evidence

24 The plan for the north tower of St Stephen's, Cathedral, Vienna, showing four superimposed levels. A medieval mason would have had no difficulty in interpreting its meaning.

25 *Left* One of the original fourteenth-century drawings for the west façade of Cologne Cathedral (built in the nineteenth century partly to these plans). The drawing, 4 m high, is made on eleven parchment membranes, and is a studio, rather than a working, drawing.

26 *Above* Masons' templates, used to define the shapes of the mouldings, were designed by the master mason and can be regarded as his personal signature.

27 Detail of a drawing made in about 1360 of the central part of the façade of Strasbourg Cathedral. Drawn with inks on parchment, it is beautifully finished with colours and shading, and was clearly not intended as a working plan.

of a completely different kind of drawing: those that actually assisted the building process. In 1344 drawings were taken to the quarry so that stones could be chosen for the transverse arch over the western rose window, and in 1495 Jehan Garnache and Colas Savetier were drawing tracery and making templates to be sent for the stones to be cut at the quarry of Tonnerre. Templates were the basis of stone cutting, providing the shapes to which the various faces were to be chiselled to make voussoirs, bases, pier sections and vault ribs, the hallmark of the master mason. William of Sens is described as delivering 'moulds' at Canterbury; a later glimpse shows Master Thomas at St Stephen's Chapel, Westminster, in 1331, designing the templates for the next

stage of the work. On this occasion he is said to be *in trasura*, in the tracing house, a feature of the lodge that is well documented elsewhere: Ulrich von Ensingen had one at Strasbourg, and at Exeter it was situated near the masons' hostel. In the tracing house the master mason worked either on boards set up on trestles or on a specially prepared plaster surface, a tracing floor.

Medieval plaster tracing floors survive at Wells Cathedral and York Minster. The Wells tracing floor is in a room over the north nave porch, which the masons must have commandeered for their use; at York it is in the L-shaped room on the first floor of the vestibule to the chapter house, built from about the 1280s, a room fitted up for the masons with a fireplace

and garderobe (and where the post-medieval templates still hang). The plaster surface is *c.*7 m x 4 m; it is covered in incised lines, among which can be identified profiles of mouldings and designs for tracery, including a full-scale design for the tracery of the choir aisle windows of the Minster, which date from the 1360s. [29] [28]

The design is drawn as a two-dimensional orthogonal projection in double outline. Its purpose was to provide guidelines for the wooden patterns that would then be cut for the shapes in the tracery head. Jacob, the master mason at Xanten in 1302, is recorded as making a wooden model of a window, presumably following just such a procedure. The design does not give the cross-sections of the mouldings, which would require their own templates [30]

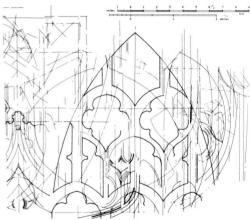

28 and **29** The choir aisle windows of York Minster (left) and the full-scale design for the tracery pattern (above) which was set out in the plaster tracing floor used by the masons in the room over the chapter house vestibule.

30 Wooden patterns for the main outlines of tracery, which would be taken from the drawings made in the tracing house.

and have separate drawings. Tracing floors could be made wherever it was convenient. At Troyes they made plaster surfaces as they were needed over redundant parts of the building such as the vaults of chapels. A drawing similar to the one at York survives at Soissons Cathedral, incised into the stone of a floor in the north-west tower; at Narbonne Cathedral the plan of one of the main piers is incised into the floor of the axial chapel. Designs were also occasionally incised on walls, but these would be difficult to work from. Loose pieces of stone were handy for small sketches, as at St John's Hospital, Cambridge, where the design of the east window was drawn small-scale on a piece of stone that was subsequently incorporated into the window itself.

The templates were cut out of board or, if they were to be taken to the quarry, canvas, parchment or reinforced paper. The template provided the outline and setting marks to guide the cutting mason, but, to judge from the commentary under sketches of profiles in Villard's *Portfolio*, he was also given verbal guidance, with a developed terminology for ribs, transverse arches and other mouldings.

Surviving tracing floors show only details. The ground-plan was drawn out on the building site; parts needing complicated calculation such as a polygonal chevet or a spiral staircase could be worked out elsewhere and transposed. The number of storeys and height of the elevation were decided between the master mason and the patron, but only the details would need to be fully worked out.

Written evidence of masonic design methods is contained in a series of instruction manuals and sketchbooks made mostly in Germany, except for a treatise on vault design written by the Spanish architect Rodrigo Gil de Hontañon. The most famous (and to us the most useful) booklets are those written by the masons Mathes Roriczer and Lorenz Lechler, which give detailed instructions on various design techniques. What is odd about all these books, however, is the date. They first appeared very late in the fifteenth century and continued to be produced well into the sixteenth. There seems to be little doubt that their contents reflect a long tradition: there are hints of the same techniques in Villard's *Portfolio*, and the laconic nature of much of the advice presupposes a degree of knowledge taken for granted. Why, therefore, after centuries of verbal transmission, was it suddenly thought desirable to write it all down? Given the date, it is possible that these books are a primitive response to the writings on architecture of Italians such as Leone Battista Alberti, whose treatise *De re aedificatoria* had been circulating in manuscript since the 1450s, before appearing in print in 1485. Although the disorganised and scrappy efforts of the northern masons are far removed from the polished certainties of Florentine humanism, there may well be a connection between the two. The date and context of these booklets should be borne in mind for another reason: Lechler's *Instructions* to his son Moritz are applied to the relatively simple structure of the late medieval German hall church, which presented far fewer design problems than a thirteenth-century French cathedral in the Rayonnant style, and we should be wary of applying everything in the booklets to the earlier period.

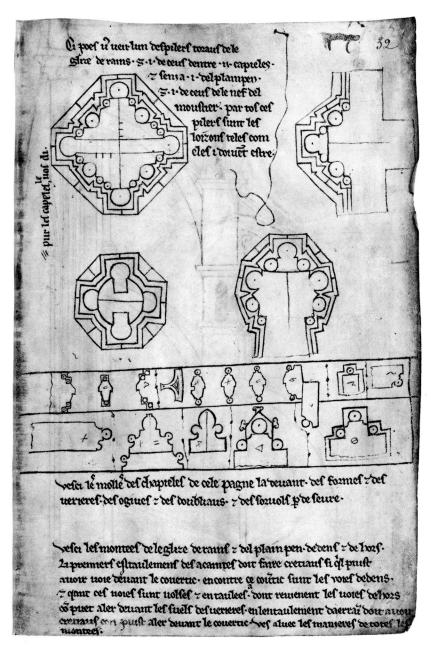

31 A page from the thirteenth-century *Portfolio* of sketches by Villard de Honnecourt showing profiles of mouldings.

Nevertheless, the writings of Roriczer and Lechler give us valuable clues to the ways in which the master mason deployed his drawing instruments, the straightedge, compasses and square. The basis of the design was so-called constructive geometry, the manipulation of squares, circles and triangles to produce lines and points from which the details could be established. These were used either as geometric figures or to achieve a set of proportional ratios that could be used as related linear measurements. Despite the fact that Euclid's *Elements* were translated in the twelfth century and late medieval masons themselves cited Euclid as some sort of legendary hero, masonic geometry was not Euclidian, even though the word 'geometrie' appears in masonic writings. No mason needed to know the theoretical basis of what he was doing, nor did he need to demonstrate that his solution was mathematically correct. What he did need to know was how to manipulate the figures to achieve the desired result. The ancestry of the method seems rather to lie in the traditions of Roman builders and surveyors, which passed unbroken from Late Antiquity, using the same methods with the same practical application, to be taught to aspiring master masons in the lodge.

The two basic figures, apart from the circle, were the triangle and the square, hence the references to construction *ad triangulum* and *ad quadratum*. The cross-section of Bourges Cathedral, for example, is set out *ad triangulum*, and much of the controversy over Milan Cathedral, *c.* 1400, was devoted to the question of whether the building should be based on a triangle or a square. The proportions of the façade of the Palazzo Sansedoni, built in Siena *c.* 1340, were based on the combined use of a square and an equilateral triangle drawn on its base. Mathes Roriczer's *Booklet on Pinnacles* gives instructions for designing a pinnacle by rotating squares to generate smaller squares in proportion; but his *Geometria Deutsch* is devoted to the equally important circle and irregular polygon, telling how, by following a series of given steps, you can draw polygons up to the dodecagon, find the circumference of a circle or

32 A portrait of Mathes Roriczer by Hans Holbein the Elder. Roriczer was the author of several booklets written in the late fifteenth century giving instructions on how to set out plans and details of buildings.

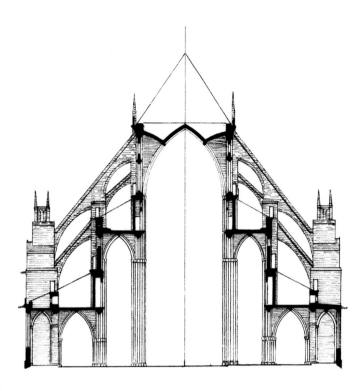

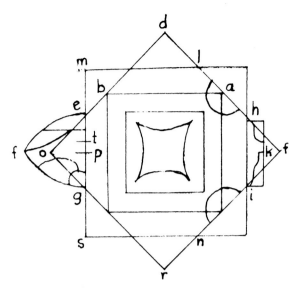

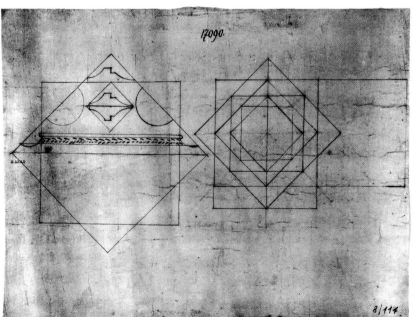

33 *Left* The cross-sections of buildings were often based on either the square (*ad quadratum*) or the triangle (*ad triangulum*). Bourges Cathedral is based on the triangle.

34 *Above* A drawing from Mathes Roriczer's late fifteenth-century *Booklet on Pinnacles*, which shows how to rotate squares to generate smaller squares in proportion, and how to use the same squares to draw the profiles of the mouldings.

35 *Left* A drawing in Vienna of rotated squares, with smaller squares and circles based on their proportions. The profile of a window mullion is contained in the small square.

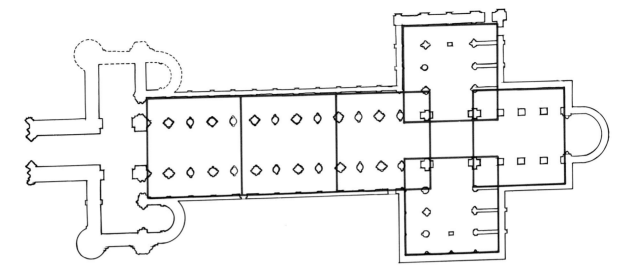

the centre of an arc, all with the dividers and straightedge, without recourse to mathematical calculations. A drawing in Vienna shows window mullions of related proportions inscribed within rotated squares, the first of which would be the module for the whole building. Lechler's *Instructions* are clear on this point: the module might be a square derived from the width of the choir, for example, and all details would be generated from it.

That in 1516 Lechler was expounding a time-honoured method can be demonstrated from the late eleventh-century Anglo-Norman ground-plan of Ely Cathedral. The interior of the choir is a square, with the width equal to the distance from the crossing arch to the chord of the apse. Using the choir square as a module as Lechler prescribes, we find the following: the nave from the west façade (excluding the later west transept) to the west crossing pier comprises three squares, and the east-west depth of the transept is one square, which overlaps the east nave and choir squares. This principle of overlap was important in locking the dimensions securely together. The transept arms are also squares, taken from inside the crossing piers. The major dimensions of the plan have thus been related and accounted for in six squares.

The smaller elements, however, are arrived

at by using the square in a different way. A square can be used to generate rectangles, the commonest in medieval architecture being generated either from the diagonal of half a square, which is the Golden Section, or from the diagonal of a complete square; here the square stands to the baseline of the rectangle in a proportion of one to the square root of two (1:1.414). These proportions, easy to produce and to remember as a principle, were often used to establish the basic dimensions, in particular the related proportions of parts of buildings — for example, the height of the arcade to that of the triforium. At Ely a square based on the width of the main vessel generates the dimensions of the arcade wall and the piers in a sequence of $\sqrt{2}$ proportional relationships: the main vessel is twice the width of the aisle, which is $\sqrt{2}$ times the distance between the aisle responds, which is $\sqrt{2}$ times the depth of the piers, which is $\sqrt{2}$ times the width of the arcade wall. These dimensions could be arrived at by halving and rotating squares; the fact that they are based on irrational numbers is of no consequence because they are set up without mathematics. The simple rule of thumb, once learnt, could be applied anywhere, and, as Lechler says, the prescriptions allow for much variation.

The methods could be used in different

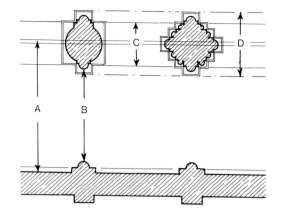

37 A system of proportions was used serially to enable the details of the building to be established without fuss. In the nave of Ely Cathedral, the widths of the main arcade, piers and aisles are related on a series of √2 proportions.

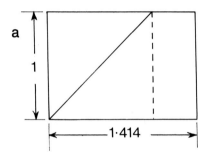
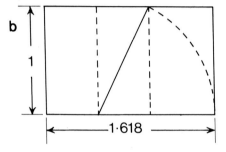

38 The linear proportions of (a) one to the square root of two and (b) the Golden Section can be drawn without mathematical calculations, by employing the square and compasses, both commonly used by masons.

combinations. For example, while the arcs of many window heads are based on an equilateral triangle or struck from points on the mullions, the choir aisle windows of York Minster, which are drawn out on the tracing floor, are among those whose radius is √2 times the width of the window. Elements in the tracery pattern are in a √2 proportional relationship to the baseline.

It was not always necessary to manipulate geometric figures to decide relative dimensions. The most commonly used proportional ratios, those based on √2, √3 and the Golden Section, were also known by their sequences of numerical approximations, which occur often enough in existing buildings for us to be reasonably certain that they were used in that form. The usual √2 series are 5:7:10, 12:17:24, 70:99:140 and multiples of these, with the numbers doubling each time; and the Golden Sec-

tion was expressed in the so-called Fibonacci series 1:2:3:5:8:13:21, etc., where the two previous numbers are added together to make the next. Once the basic unit of measurement had been established (almost everywhere closely approximating to the foot), the dimensions could be generated, the size of the building depending on the size of the basic unit. In the fourteenth-century choir of Howden Minster [39] the 12:17:24 ratio is clearly used, based on a bay length of 17 ft 3 in (5.18 m) which is also the height of the arcade and of the east window arch. The arch springs 24 ft (7.2 m) from the floor. This shows the principle of interlocking dimensions observed at Ely. The full height of the combined triforium and clerestory is 17 ft 6 in (5.25 m), and the distance from the triforium floor to the spring of the inner arch is 12 ft 3 in (3.68 m). These proportional relationships can, therefore, be established either geometrically or numerically; they were infinitely versatile and their use exemplifies the flexible pragmatism exhibited at every stage of the building process.

According to the Regensburg Ordinances, a mason had to be able to take the elevation from the ground plan. This may mean no more than the application of the kind of linked proportions seen at, for instance, Howden, but it may be significant that such requirements were codified only at a time when vault patterns were becoming extremely complicated, and an intricate design drawn in two dimensions had to be projected in three to calculate the correct curvature of the ribs. Lechler's *Instructions* give an exceedingly obscure explanation of how to do this, luckily clarified by an illustration in a [40] later copy of his work. The whole design was drawn out full-scale, and the height of the vault at its apex was decided. Taking the shortest route, the lengths of the ribs between the springers and the keystone were added together to form a baseline from which a quadrant was struck to form the principal arc from which all the curvatures were derived. Verticals taken from the rib lengths marked on the baseline intersected the arc, and the curvature of, for instance, rib A was that of the arc between A and B. The next step, shown in an early

sixteenth-century plan for a vault in Strasbourg Cathedral, shows that ribs of the same curvature and length were marked on a placement plan, so that once cut they were effectively interchangeable. A model produced from the drawing of a vault projection in the so-called *Dresden Sketchbook* has shown that the method works, but whether it was applied to Early and High Gothic vaults from the twelfth to the fourteenth centuries has yet to be demonstrated.

CONSTRUCTION

Around 1200 Bishop Marshall of Exeter 'finished the building according to the Plan and Foundation that his predecessors had laid'. Whether the foundations for the whole building had been dug all at once is doubtful,

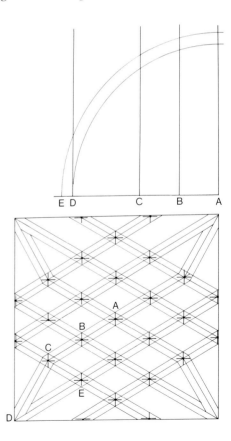

39 The choir elevation of Howden Church, Humberside, was established by a series of √2 proportions relating the arcades, east window and clerestory to the length of a bay (reconstruction by E. Sharpe).

40 *Right* The construction of vaulting ribs in the late Gothic period. To set the correct curvature, the lengths of each section of rib between joins were drawn out as a continuous line, and a curve struck to form the principal arc, from which the curvatures of the individual ribs were then taken. It has been shown to work on a small scale model.

but the ground-plan had been fully laid out. It was set out on the ground with poles, ropes, cord and lime to mark the edges and lines of the interior. Foundations were dug down to bedrock if possible, and on a marshy site wooden piles would be sunk. Medieval foundations, where they are known, vary in relation to the superstructure: at Beauvais they are based on a chalk bedrock, descending possibly 10 m in stepped platforms, with sleeper walls running between the piers; at Reims they are 4-5 m wide and 9 m deep; and at Amiens, which is a lower building than Beauvais, they are 15 m deep. A later building could be founded on the footings of its predecessor, as at the Minsters of York and Ripon, where the arcades of the Gothic naves are built on the foundations of the Anglo-Norman outer walls. Although the foundations of later buildings were often packed with spoil from an earlier one (a fine Romanesque capital was discovered in the foundations of the High Gothic cathedral of Soissons), the material was normally carefully chosen, as can be seen from contracts that specify the type of stone to be used. The foundations of the Anglo-Norman cathedral at York consisted of retaining walls enclosing an oak grillage, which was then covered with a mortared rubble core. Once dry, it was strong enough to support walls nearly 30 m high. At Troyes, however, the chalky stone used in the foundations became damp and formed a paste, seriously weakening the structure.

The choice of stone depended on the region, although good building stone could be transported great distances. Buildings were constructed either of ashlar — high quality dressed blocks of limestone, sandstone, granite or marble — or of rubble, which was also used for packing and filling. Brick is found in parts of buildings such as vaults where they wanted to use a lighter material, and it was common in regions such as the Netherlands or East Anglia, where there was little good stone; yet Norwich Cathedral, for example, is partly built of stone shipped from Caen in Normandy.

Building stones ranged in colour from almost white through cream, beige, grey and greenish to the red sandstones found in the west Midlands. With these could be used the dark, burnishable limestones known as 'marble', which were quarried at Tournai in Belgium and areas of England such as Corfe in Dorset. These were good for contrasting decorative work, in piers, shafting and vault ribs. [41] Soft stone such as the Midlands alabasters were suitable only for interior work, and both alabaster and Purbeck marble became very popular for tombs. Stone was chosen for its suitability for a particular function or feature: at Exeter Cathedral, which called upon many quarries, traceries and spandrels were made exclusively of Salcombe stone. Ideally the patron or the administration owned the quarries, and sometimes the use of a quarry was granted by a local family, such as the Vavasours of Yorkshire, who gave the York Minster authorities access to their quarry at Tadcaster. Otherwise stone had to be bought: at Exeter it was bought during periods of affluence and stockpiled for future use.

The relation between the building works and the quarry was close, the master mason going to the quarry frequently to inspect the stone beds and provide the templates for the stones that were to be worked there rather than on the site. Except for detailed mouldings and final trimmings, much of the stone was cut to size at the quarry; many stones are soft on first exposure to the air, and it was in any case cheaper to transport cut stone. Blocks and quoins (corner stones) were supplied ready cut to many sites, including Caernarfon Castle, and quarry identification marks have been found on blocks from the big French quarries such as Caen and Tonnerre. Owing to the hardness of Purbeck stone and its shallow beds, the marblers of Corfe did much of the cutting themselves, sometimes selling decorative details and tombs ready-made to their own templates: small decorative marble bases, identical both in size and profile, have been noted on securely dated objects that are twenty years and two hundred miles apart. They could also cut to an agreed template, as did Canons of Corfe when they provided the main piers and gallery colonnettes for Exeter Cathedral. In their final, itemised account of 1332, each pier [42] cost £10.16s, expensive at the time.

Owing to its cost, the supply and transport of stone required careful organisation. One way to reduce the expense was to reuse material from earlier buildings, as at St Albans in the late eleventh century, where the abbot stockpiled bricks from the nearby Roman site of Verulamium for use in the new building. Otherwise the quarry was often as near as possible to the site itself: the castles of Coucy and Château-Gaillard in France were built of stone quarried from the rocks on which they stand. Sometimes the organisation was the responsibility of the administration, at others it was contracted out. As early as the 1170s William of Sens seems to have been acting as a supplier, but the heyday of the mason contractor really began in the thirteenth century. In the 1300s the Exeter Cathedral authorities employed a quarryman, Golofre, solely to organise supply and transport from various quarries, but by 1330 the expense of maintaining horses, carts and the roads themselves had forced them to contract out the entire operation.

As transport over land was inordinately expensive the quarry would ideally be accessible by water. Water transport was considered important enough at Rievaulx Abbey for a special canal to be dug. There were specifically designated wharves for landing stone brought up the River Ouse from Tadcaster to York, and upriver from Beer and Salcombe to Exeter. The Regensburg authorities had their own boat. For land transport carts and draught animals had to be rented, and the journey could take a long time: seventeen days were needed for ten carts, each pulled by eight horses, to carry the alabaster retable sent from Notting-

41 Contrasting 'marbles' (dark limestones that would take a high polish) were used for decorative columns and foliage, as here at Salisbury Cathedral in about 1230.

42 *Left* The piers and colonnettes of Exeter Cathedral were made by the Purbeck marbler William Canon and his son, who supplied the Cathedral for more than twenty years.

43 *Opposite* Labourers unloading stone from a boat. Transport over land was so expensive that, wherever possible, stone was carried by water. Some cathedral authorities, such as Regensburg, had their own boat. At Exeter and York there were special wharves where the stone was unloaded.

43

ham to Windsor in 1367. The expense was, therefore, very great. Stone bought at Huddlestone in 1415 for York Minster cost £9.14s, but its carriage was more than twice that amount. Building authorities were nevertheless undeterred by cost if a particular stone was preferred. Norwich was only one of many sites in England that imported Caen stone, and stone was brought 60 km along the Roman road from Tonnerre to Troyes, as the nearer quarries, which were sometimes used, yielded inferior stone.

The final cutting was done at the bankers in the lodge and, whenever possible, stones were put in place fully moulded. Although there is some evidence of carving *in situ*, it was not usual; masons disliked having to do intricate work at high levels, and at Milan in 1485 those who did foliage or figure carving on the scaffolding were paid more than those who worked on the ground. The stone was cut with saws, axes, chisels and drills, all of which needed constant resharpening, an item that featured heavily in the building accounts: at Ely there are separate entries for sharpening the axes of the sacrist's men (at work on the octagon) and the bishop's men (a different team, working on the new choir bays). Individual stones frequently carry incised symbols known as masons' marks; these were [45] identification marks of doubtful function, but probably used initially in task work so that each mason's contribution could be precisely calculated, and also perhaps for quality control. Marks were also used for positioning, as can be seen on the statue of Joseph on the west [44] front of Reims Cathedral, and setting marks were put on stones to guide cutting masons.

The mortar, two parts sand to one part lime, was mixed on the site, and the stones carried piece by piece in baskets, wheelbarrows, on the shoulders (protected by leather hoods), or on two-man trays that could then be raised by crane or windlass The mason-setters mortared [47] the stones in with trowels. Verticals were tested with plumblines or squares, which were both among the instruments, along with compasses [46] and straightedge, that the master mason was expected to provide for himself. They were

44 *Above* A setting mark, incised on the stone, indicated where a statue should be placed, and is seen here behind the figure of Joseph on Reims Cathedral.

45 *Left* The function of the mason's mark, a small device scratched on individual stones, is not fully understood. It was an identification mark, perhaps originally used in task work where a mason was paid according to the amount of work he did.

46 Testing the verticals with a plumbline, a treasured item of the master mason's equipment which he was expected to provide for himself. Other tools seen in this picture, such as the wheelbarrow, were provided by the building authorities.

evidently valued, and Ulrich von Ensingen bequeathed his to the Strasbourg lodge.

At Canterbury Cathedral, where the outside walls had been left relatively unscathed by the fire, the new choir was built within the shell [48] of the old, in this instance from the main transept eastwards. The order of building usually made provision to keep the old structure until there was enough of the new one for altars to [49] come into use. Thus work almost always proceeded from outside inwards, and often from east to west, to enable the liturgically important part to be finished first. Monastery churches were often built from the transept

adjoining the monastic buildings (usually the south), but there were no rules. Bourges Cathedral followed what we regard as the convention, but Chartres was apparently built from the crossing in both directions at once, and Amiens Cathedral was started at the west end because a parish church on the proposed site of the choir was to be kept as long as possible.

It is from Gervase of Canterbury that we gain the earliest clear insights into the order of building. Suger's account of Saint-Denis was written some seventy years before, but apart from the odd remark that helps us to make inferences about certain structural matters, it

tells us nothing about the architecture. As far as the architecture of Canterbury was concerned, Gervase himself was interested only in the main elevation and the vault that provided such a startling contrast to their predecessors; we learn nothing from him about the buttresses, roofing, the aisles or the obvious changes of design. Yet it is clear from the surviving structure that the information he does give is quite accurate. Building proceeded eastwards bay by bay, but William of Sens placed several pairs of piers before he built any of the vaults, so that the piers always kept well ahead of the vaulting programme. According to Gervase, two or three aisle bays were the first to be vaulted: this is quite correct, as the aisle vaults provide support to the wall above the main arcade, and they would have to be put in before the latter was built. Only after that could the main vaults be put in place. By the time of William's fall in 1178 all the choir piers were in position, but several bays of high vaulting remained to be done. We must presume that the timber roof over the vaults had been set up truss by truss before the stone vaults were built. This was the normal procedure, protecting both the workers and the building from the weather. The urgent necessity for weatherproofing can be seen vividly in the building accounts of Troyes, where, owing to a protracted building campaign lasting more than two centuries and efforts at economy that made them use an absorbent, chalky stone, there was a perpetual need to maintain and renew parts of the unfinished building. Rain came in through poor guttering, and frost penetrated exposed piers. Thatching the walls in winter afforded some protection, but if building ceased for any length of time deterioration was inevitable.

Building proceeded bay by bay in such a manner that if work did stop the structure would hold. It was normal, for instance, when building the crossing, to put up a bay beyond it to act as a prop. If there was no change in the size and source of the individual ashlars or the design of the mouldings, there need not be any sign that there was a pause in construction. Some buildings show very clear breaks, others

Canterbury Cathedral

The eastern arm in the summer of 1175, prepared for the rebuilding work to start.

© John Atherton Bowen 1989

47 *Opposite* Masons using trowels to mortar the stone. At the bottom of the picture a mason cuts stone with a hammer and chisel, while his companion wields a set square.

48 *Above* A medieval building was often the replacement of an earlier one, parts of which could be incorporated in the new work. At Canterbury Cathedral in the late twelfth century the new choir was built within the shell of its burnt predecessor.

49 Medieval building construction, showing the new work being added to the old, and masons building the outside walls.

50 *Left* Arches and vaults were constructed over wooden centering, which held the stones in place until they had settled and the mortar set. These are the vaults of Soissons Cathedral being rebuilt after World War I.

51 *Below left* Tie-bars in the choir aisles of Westminster Abbey which were used to brace the structures.

52 *Below* Stones used for the piers of Amiens Cathedral in the thirteenth century. Made of identical pieces that could interlock, these could be ordered and cut well in advance of being set in place.

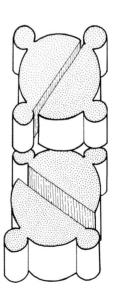

53 There were various forms of medieval scaffolding. Here the masons use platforms attached to the building by putlog holes and reached by ladders and staircases.

do not. There was no rule about the quantity of stone to be prepared in advance, and this almost certainly depended on the amount of money available. At Troyes they ordered the stone for one pier at a time, whereas at Exeter the Corfe marblers seem to have supplied several piers at once, or at any rate to have known that a large number would be needed. At Amiens and some other sites in France the pier stones were cut in regular, interlocking courses that were clearly prefabricated to a pattern, indicating that the number required was planned and ordered from the start.

The arches of the main arcade, windows, doorways and vaults were built over centering, usually wooden framing cut to the exact shape of the arch, over which the voussoirs (arch stones) would be set. The centering was left in place until the mortar had dried and the arch could hold itself together. There is evidence as

54 A building could be completely covered in scaffolding of wooden poles lashed together.

late as 1496 at Troyes that earth was used as centering, heaped up to the shape of the vault webs, but we do not know how common this was. The building could also be held together on a framework of wooden, sometimes metal, tie-bars, which were embedded in the piers at the base of the arches. Tie-bars survive in the thirteenth-century choir aisles of Westminster Abbey, and remains of them were found during restoration work at Soissons Cathedral. [50]

The higher they went, the greater the need for scaffolding, ladders and machines for hauling stone. Scaffolding had to be made of wood, [53,54] and although some medieval illustrations depict buildings encased in it, most show scaffolding being used rather sparingly. The building itself provided access in the staircases and passages that were built into it as the walls rose, and when platforms were needed they were often built out on scaffolding poles projecting horizontally from putlog holes that were left in the wall for this purpose. Ladders of various kinds are shown, and also walkways made of [55,58] withies (attested in the records) which provided a regular slope that clearly made carriage easier. The putlog holes are still visible in the walls of the castles of Conwy and Harlech, [56] inclined on the curtain wall and spiralling on the towers. Cranes and windlasses were built into the upper levels for winding up the stones in baskets or trugs, or, by the late Middle Ages, [59] clutched by large metal pincers. The windlass [57] used in building the spire of Salisbury Cathedral in the early fourteenth century is still in place, together with the 'tree' of wooden scaffolding inside the spire, which, having helped with the construction, now helps to brace the stonework. The crane left looming over Cologne Cathedral when building was abandoned in the fourteenth century was still a famous part of the skyline in the early sixteenth. Wherever possible the masons stood on the greater safety of the walls themselves, [60] but accidents did happen, as we have seen, and not always through human carelessness. The building itself carried its own dangers, as at Troyes in 1530, when Colin Millet was killed by the fall of a flying buttress that failed when its centering was removed.

55 *Opposite, top* Masons, with hods of mortar on their shoulders, use ladders to gain access to the building.

56 *Opposite,, bottom left* The walkways were attached to the building by putlog holes. A series of these is arranged in a spiral round the gatehouse towers of Harlech Castle.

57 *Opposite, bottom right* The huge windlass, or hoist, used in building the spire of Salisbury Cathedral in the fourteenth century, is still in place today.

58 *Right* Safer than ladders were walkways made of withies; the purchase of withies often noted in building accounts.

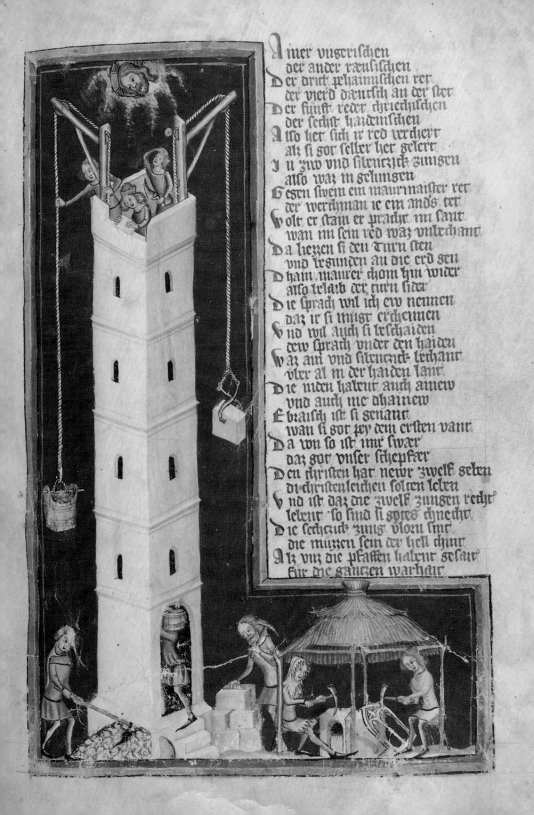

59 *Left* Stone was lifted to the upper parts of the building either in baskets or in giant pincers, operated by a hoist.

60 *Opposite* The passages, spiral staircases and thick walls of a medieval building could be used by the masons for access to the unfinished upper levels. Scaffolding was far less safe, as William of Sens found to his cost at Canterbury in 1178 (see page 17).

er selle turn als ich laz
W anne der geslechte na der zal
A ls vil waz über al.
A ls ich hie noe gesprochen han
M ir hait die schrift vns kunt getan
D az funfzehen kunne schar
aphetes kunne gebar
em der reine gute man
elen unde zwentzich sune gewan.

ie wuescaft die in wande
D ie vppighen hohfart
D er ir dumheit zu rade wart-

STRUCTURE AND STRUCTURAL THEORY

It may seem rather odd that even in the six-teenth century, with four hundred years' cumulative experience, masons could build a flying buttress that was not structurally sound; but perhaps it is no odder than the inability of car manufacturers even now to make a perfect gearbox. A large medieval building is, to modern eyes, a breathtaking triumph of skill over probability. A Gothic great church in particular looks at once dangerously fragile for its size and heavy enough to defy all the laws of structural stability. Yet surprisingly few medieval buildings fell; towers sometimes collapsed, but the ability of a tower to withstand the pull of gravity is daily demonstrated at Pisa, where 61 the bell-tower of the cathedral is only now, after eight hundred years of leaning, giving real cause for concern.

The documentary evidence from the cathedrals of Troyes and Milan disconcertingly shows that any coherent advanced plan was in practice ignored, and medieval buildings could apparently withstand substantial alterations to the fabric both during construction and after an interval of many years. These alterations might just be superficial changes of detail — such as the triforium design of Wells Cathedral or the pier at Canterbury, whose shape was changed half-way up to accommodate 62 changes further east — or slightly more serious — such as in late fourteenth-century Winchester, where part of the Anglo-Norman 63 masonry was hacked away for the nave to be recased in Perpendicular mouldings. The mismatched footings and superstructure in the choir of Tewkesbury Abbey or the contrivances in the upper storeys of Lincoln Cathedral perhaps count as hasty compensation for miscalculation rather than actual changes, while other places show ideas about structure

61 With proper foundations a masonry building is stable and it can survive for centuries, even on a marshy site, as demonstrated by the twelfth-century Leaning Tower of Pisa.

developing as the building proceeds, as with the vaults of Durham Cathedral, where the design was refined as they went along. Far more radical assaults could, however, be made on the structure: at York Minster they switched round pairs of arches beside the crossing piers, and when in the thirteenth century the super-structure of the choir of Saint-Denis was re-built, they underpinned the arches and capitals of the main arcade in order to insert new piers while preserving the ambulatory and its vault-ing. The discussions held at Milan at the turn of the fourteenth and fifteenth centuries reveal that they could safely change their minds about the proposed height and proportions of the cathedral when it was already half-built, al-though when this had been tried at Beauvais in the mid-thirteenth century disaster had ensued.

Stone is, evidently, a stable material. In any realistic context it will not crush under its own weight, and after an initial period of settlement during which the parts of the building find equilibrium, and providing there is no external interference such as an earthquake or a drop in the water-table (which will affect the founda-tions), the building will remain in a constant state. The main arms of the church support themselves, aisles against the main vessel, the inner ends against the crossing, the exposed ends buttressed, often with towers. In a Gothic building the greatest threat to stability is the thrust engendered by the stone vault and the timber roof above it. A high, thin building will be heavier and more subject to the forces en-gendered by strong winds; but as long as the lines of thrust can be carried safely to the ground within the encasing masonry all should be well.

The thrusts are absorbed by buttresses, and buttressing the high vaults of a Gothic great church is the greatest structural problem that any builder has had to confront. A Gothic church seems to us to be concentrated inwards,

62 Changes in design could be made up until the last minute: a pier at Canterbury Cathedral was changed halfway up from octagonal to circular.

R.WILLIS del

63 A medieval building is not always what it seems: the Perpendicular-style nave of Winchester Cathedral consists of a moulded facing applied to the original Norman core.

the greatest aesthetic and emotional effect of arches and stained glass being experienced inside the building. This was clearly a deliberate aim, but its achievement was undoubtedly helped by the fact that vaults thrust downwards and outwards, so that counteracting forces have to be put on the exterior, leaving the interior spaces free and uncluttered.

An arched flying buttress is necessary only on an aisled building, where the thrusts have to be taken out over the aisle to the pier-buttress at the perimeter. An arched buttress of this type is found as early as the fourth century, in the Basilica of Maxentius in the Forum in Rome, which has massive groin vaults supported at least partly by arched buttresses. Until about the middle of the twelfth century buttressing walls could be concealed under the lean-to roofs of the aisles, but with the increasing height of individual storeys after that date the vaults began to spring from higher up, and the buttresses had to be exposed above the aisle roofs. For this, as in the Basilica of Maxentius, an arch was lighter in weight, less wasteful of stone, just as efficient and, we presume, aesthetically more pleasing. Certainly, once the flying buttress had been adopted, builders went to great pains to refine its appearance.

The upper wall beneath a stone vault is 64 extremely vulnerable. Barrel vaults, which are simply tunnels, are unsatisfactory because they exert pressure evenly over their whole length, and it can be dangerous to cut windows in the walls. The advantage of the groin vault, which is the equivalent of intersecting barrels, is that the four creases formed by the intersection collect and transmit the thrusts, so that groins need to be supported mainly at these points. Much loading is taken off the walls, which can be opened for arches or windows. The rib vault acts in essentially the same way, but is more versatile. Any vault is built over supporting centering, but the webs of a groin vault are difficult to assemble over any but a square bay. In an early Gothic rib vault the ribs were built first, and if necessary separately, with different lengths and curvatures, locked by the central keystone, as expounded by Ger-

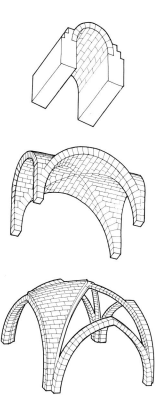

64 The different types of vault used from Roman times into the Middle Ages: *top* barrel; *middle* groin (two intersecting barrels); *bottom* rib (a developed form of groin vault with the cross arches on which it is based exposed on the underside).

vase. The straight bays could now be rectangular, and over an ambulatory there could be three or five ribs in each turning bay. The webs, at first made of mortared rubble and later of jointed masonry, were filled in to the required shape over the ribs, leaving them exposed. The vault webs are shell structures, held together by their own curvature and weak only at the point where they are deeply folded, but they are supported there by the ribs. Once the webs have settled, the ribs and the webs support themselves independently of each other, as has been demonstrated in those buildings where, through accident or bombing, the ribs have fallen but the webs remained intact. Suger describes how, during the building of Saint-Denis, the newly built ribs, standing unsupported and as yet without webs, were able to withstand a violent wind. The rib is thus convenient for construction, and remains thereafter as a valuable aesthetic device.

The thrusts being carried down the transverse arches and the creases behind the ribs are absorbed into the wall just above the springing. The vault therefore exerts maximum pressure at this point. From the early thirteenth century the efficiency of this area was greatly improved by the development of the *tas-de-charge*, a set of through stones in squared masonry that formed the lowest sections of the ribs and transverse arches and extended back into the wall itself. Cutting the stones required considerable skill in setting-out, but the *tas-de-charge* meant that cutting the springers of several ribs from a single stone added to their strength and stability, and the lowest courses of the vault could be built without centering. The *tas-de-charge* conveyed the vault thrusts through the wall to the head of the arched flier that was propped against the building at that point. The thrusts then continued down the arch to the outer pier-buttress, and as long as the arch was shaped to contain the line of thrust, the flier would do its job. Drawn sections of Gothic churches show that the heads of the fliers are positioned more or less where they should be (they failed at Amiens because they were not); the upper tier, placed under the eaves, is there to absorb the thrusts engendered by the timber-

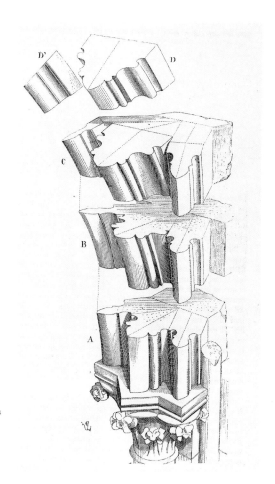

65 The *tas-de-charge* is a series of through-stones forming the lower levels of the vault, which extend back into the wall itself, locking the vault into position.

framed roof. Pinnacles on the roofline or pier-buttresses provide vertical pressure that pins the buttresses and helps to prevent outward bend. The building is clamped together by a series of devices that act and counteract, and the decorative qualities, particularly of Late Gothic buttresses and pinnacles, should not blind us to their essential function.

How much of this was known to medieval masons is one of the most tantalising questions because it cannot definitely be answered. That their buildings remain standing after so many centuries surely suggests that they knew what they were doing, but contemporary written sources indicate that they had no structural theory of a kind that a modern structural engineer would recognise. Medieval masons had no means of calculating the amount of buttressing required by any particular design, and seem to have discovered the margins of safety through observation and experience; they were additionally fortunate in that the proportions to which they built happened to lie within the necessary limits of stability. Their tendency was, if anything, to err on the side of safety and provide more buttressing than engineers now know to be necessary. The actual weight of the vault could be reduced by using light materials such as tufa (Canterbury) or brick (Beverley Minster). English masons persisted for over two centuries with the Anglo-Norman thick wall structure, where a mortared rubble fill is encased in ashlar. This, while producing walls over 3 m thick and capable of absorbing the thrusts of a stone vault, prevented them from building the very high, thin Gothic structures of France. The most celebrated occasion on which we know that masonic instinct failed was the collapse of Beauvais Cathedral in 1284. This has been plausibly explained by a change to a new design that required far more buttressing, which was provided to the new work but not where the new overlapped the old. There the insufficiently buttressed, attenuated piers bent fatally inwards. It is interesting that Heinrich Parler's proposal of 1392 for Milan Cathedral, which would have created a similar discrepancy in height between the aisles and the main vessel, with the same weakness, was comprehensively rejected by the Italians and Heinrich himself was dismissed.

Surviving records reveal that both patrons and masons became deeply anxious about structural questions. It was quite usual to hold an 'Expertise', that is, a conference comprising a number of outside masters, to inspect and advise on faults that had developed in old buildings, as at Chartres in 1316, or on a new building campaign that seemed to be going awry. In late medieval Spain the process was supervised from the start by a *junta*, or council, of consulting architects. In 1174 the monks of Canterbury consulted several masters before appointing William of Sens (who came nearest to telling them what they wanted to hear). At Troyes, where several consultations took place over the years, the chapter (and sometimes the bishop) were closely involved in the final decision; in 1401 they sought the advice of two different masters before making up their minds.

When in 1416 Guillermo Boffiy, the master mason of Girona Cathedral, designed a single-cell nave requiring a vault of 73 ft (22 m) span, [66] the authorities were so alarmed that they called in eleven masters, questioning each individually as to the feasibility of Boffiy's plan. The masters unanimously supported Boffiy and, as a tribute to their faith, his astonishing design survives to this day, making Girona one of the truly great late medieval interiors. One question that the masters were asked concerned the compatibility of the open, unified space of the nave with the three aisles of the choir. Would the proportions be acceptable? Here the masters were divided, and it is one of the few glimpses we have of contemporary ideas on proportion. The Expertise held at Siena Cathedral in 1322 is another: here, after declaring the new work to be fundamentally unsound, Lorenzo Maitani and his colleagues ended by saying: 'Item, that it should not proceed further for the old church is so well proportioned and its parts agree so well in breadth, length, and height that if anything were added to any part, it would be better instead to destroy the said church completely, wishing to bring it to the right measure for a church.'

66 The nave of Girona Cathedral, Catalonia, was designed by Guillermo Boffiy in 1416. It is vaulted by a single span of 22 m, which alarmed the authorities so much that they called an Expertise of masters to discuss it. Guillermo's design was endorsed unanimously, and he created one of the great late medieval interiors.

At the most famous Expertise of all, held at Milan around 1400, questions of structure and proportion are inextricably linked; if a building were proportionately correct, if it had 'the right measure', it would be structurally correct. Founded in 1386 by Giangaleazzo Visconti, the ruler of Milan, the new cathedral was intended to resemble the Gothic styles of northern Europe rather than the simpler buildings of Lombardy, and the masons soon ran into difficulties with setting out. Successive northern masters, Nicholas Bonaventure, Heinrich Parler of Ulm, Ulrich von Ensingen and Jean Mignot, came to act as consultants; the first three were rapidly dismissed or left of their own accord, but Jean Mignot lasted a little longer, although his criticisms were just as unpopular and equally ignored. The problem for everyone was that by 1390 no one in northern Europe was building a massive church of the kind apparently envisaged by Giangaleazzo (for example, work on Cologne Cathedral had been halted), and of the consulting masters only Ulrich von Ensingen had recent experience of that kind of structure. In addition, the Italians did not like what they were told and remained determined to build the cathedral in their own way.

The discussions began as a search for the correct height of the building and the best way to achieve it: should it be set out *ad triangulum* or *ad quadratum*? By 1401, however, when Mignot gave his opinion, the talks had developed into a quarrel about practical engineering, dimensions and proportion. There were discussions between the masons themselves and the masons and the authorities; all were minuted, but in condensed form by clerks who probably did not understand much about architecture, and any consideration of the evidence has to allow for this. It does seem clear, however, that both sides believed that building should be done according to certain rules, but that they were working to different rules. The Italians emerge as much more practical: when Mignot said that the buttresses were not large enough to do their job, the Milanese retorted that the local marble was stronger than northern limestone and added that 'the weight of a buttress

67 The interior of Milan Cathedral was the subject of a notorious controversy over the proportions to which it should be built. Still standing after 600 years, it justifies the faith of the winning faction among the builders.

should follow its due order through a straight line'. If by this they meant that the lines of thrust will take the quickest route to the earth and must be encased in masonry all the way, they were showing a clear grasp of the structural behaviour of stone. Mignot was inclined to stress that there were certain agreed ways of doing things which the Milanese were ignoring, including the accepted practices of geometry. The Milanese appealed to the craft tradition, whereupon Mignot delivered the aphorism that has made him immortal: *Ars sine scientia nihil est.* By this he meant that the practice (*ars*) of masonry is nothing without theoretical knowledge (*scientia*), in this case geometry. In his view the Italians were not applying geometric principles correctly, and this would lead to a faulty building. As far as Mignot was concerned the technical and the aesthetic were one. The rules themselves, however, remain obstinately vague. The only comparable rule is that of the correct thickness of a buttress in proportion to a pier: Mignot says it should be 3:1, but the treatise of Gil de Hontañón gives 4:1 and the Milanese claimed that 1.5:1 was quite sufficient. There was evidently no more rational basis for any of these opinions than there is for rival recipes for marmalade. For the present we are obliged to conclude that established pragmatic solutions provided the safest basis for experiment, and that the pragmatism of the Milanese was fully justified, for six hundred years on Milan Cathedral stands proud as ever.

SCULPTURAL DECORATION

Medieval buildings are today largely bereft of an essential feature — the decoration to which the architecture, however interesting in itself, was the backdrop. The great illustrative programmes of stained glass, painting and sculpture have been the victims of decay, changing fashions and periods of iconoclasm; only at Chartres Cathedral, where the glazing and sculpture are still more or less intact, can we sense what must have been the medieval experience.

If architecture was the setting for sculpture,

68 Reliefs of sculptors at work, carved by Nanni di Banco at Or San Michele, Florence. They are seen carving colonnettes, capitals and figures, using drills, hammers and axes. Note the plumbline, square and compasses, associated with architects, but also used by sculptors.

the latter, despite its appearance on freestanding objects such as pulpits or tombs, and the development of figures in the round, never quite freed itself from architecture. It was revived in the eleventh century as a substitute for architectural members such as capitals and door jambs, and by the late Middle Ages, when architecture itself had become very sculptural in its effects, and in its miniature forms was invading most other works of art, the distinction between the two was frequently blurred. Blank surfaces were covered in moulded and foliate decoration, and images, theoretically detached from the structure, were usually placed in a niche or tabernacle.

The profession of stone carver was rooted in the quarry and the lodge, and it is difficult to isolate the moment at which sculptors emerged as specialists. Inscriptions by sculptors appear as early as the twelfth century (Gislebertus of Autun is the obvious example, but the Italians frequently signed their works),

and carvers of images (full-length figures) were being classified in building accounts as *imagier* or *imaginator* by the late thirteenth century. From then on there is some recognition of a figure-sculptor as a distinct being. At Exeter in 1323-4 a sculptor was specially brought from London to carve images, even though members of the regular workforce were busy carving heads for the vaulting; around 1390 the magistrates of Oxford decided that John Sampson was not being overpaid, because his skill as a freemason and carver was such that comparison with the skills of other masons was not possible. Claus Sluter, who worked for the Duke of Burgundy in about 1400, was a specialist sculptor, and in the later fifteenth century and the sixteenth sculptors were brought in to carve capitals and images at Troyes Cathedral.

The evidence seems to suggest that by about 1300 figure-sculpture — that is, the carving of images — was becoming a separate branch of the craft, for which a specialist might

be employed. This does not, however, mean that architects were not also image-makers and vice versa. What may seem clear to us was evidently far from clear either to them or to the clerks who made up the wages lists. The accounts for the crosses and tombs made in 1291-4 to commemorate Queen Eleanor, wife of Edward I, show that some of the masons were engaged in both general construction and carving statues, but Alexander of Abingdon is referred to exclusively as *imaginator*, which shows that he was regarded as a specialist figure sculptor. Alexander's Italian contemporaries, Giovanni Pisano and Arnolfo di Cambio, were both architects and sculptors, and in the later fourteenth century Raymond du Temple and the Dammartin brothers, attested architects, were making statues for the grand staircase of the Louvre. The skill of Peter Parler in Prague and Anton Pilgram in Vienna is equally that of the architect-sculptor. As architects made tombs and monumental pieces of church furniture such as screens and sedilia, it makes little sense to draw too rigid a distinction between skills. There are, however, instances in the late Middle Ages of architects and sculptors working together as a regular team. Juan Guas, master mason of S. Juan de los Reyes in Toledo, was the initiator of the so-called Hispano-Flemish style in late fifteenth-century Spain, a style dependent on the close relationship between sculpture and architecture; most of his buildings were collaborative efforts between Guas himself and the sculptor Egas Cueman. In early sixteenth-century Nuremberg buildings by the city architect Hans Beheim were often embellished by the sculptor Adam Kraft.

Sculptors, therefore, came in many guises, and their talents were employed in many different ways. The role of the patron was particularly active in the decorative scheme.

69 A sculptor carving capitals. These were usually done on the ground, but the masons depicted here would have been paid more for doing the intricate carvings from scaffolding.

70 Sculptors often signed their work. This is the signature of Gislebertus, sculptor of Autun Cathedral, incised below the feet of Christ on the Last Judgement tympanum over the west door.

71 *Above* The figures of Queen Eleanor of Castile (*d.* 1290) on the commemorative Eleanor Cross at Waltham, Essex, were carved by Alexander of Abingdon, a leading figure sculptor of his day.

72 *Left* Anton Pilgram of Vienna was, like many others, both architect and sculptor. His self-portrait appears twice in Vienna Cathedral, here on the pulpit. He is holding his compasses, and his mason's mark is on the shield above his head.

Sculptures were intricate and time-consuming, and therefore expensive, to carve, so that the patron had to decide how much he could afford. A complicated theological programme such as that on the west front of Wells Cathedral would almost certainly be worked out by the clergy, even if the sculptors supplied the models and patterns for the iconography. Even the latter is far from certain: the question of who supplied the design of a sculptural programme is as yet open. The chancel fittings, sedilia, Easter sepulchre and tomb at Heckington and Hawton were made following the same scheme within a very few years of each other but by different sculptors. Was the design chosen by the patron of Hawton after he had seen Heckington? It was clearly not being sold as a package to different churches by the Heckington sculptors, whose style has been traced to Navenby in Lincolnshire, where they produced sedilia and an Easter sepulchre to a different pattern; and Hawton, which is a reinterpretation of the Heckington idea, is by a different group.

It is also clear that despite the employment of individual image-makers, the practice of sculpture could be as collective an activity as building a wall. The work of two groups has been identified in the early fourteenth-century reliefs on the façade of Orvieto Cathedral, and within those groups several hands were successively at work on all areas, so that no single figure was the work of one sculptor. There was a decided sequence of labour, from roughing out the blocks to the final touches. The reliefs in the roughly contemporary Lady Chapel at Ely were carved in at least six styles, which were not confined to any particular part of the building. The Percy tomb at Beverley Minster, on the other hand, was made by five sculptors, each of whom carved one part and was responsible for everything in it. They were evidently under strong central control, but although two of them worked in other parts of the Minster, there is no discernible 'workshop style'.

As usual, working methods were adapted to the demands of the individual site. At least some of the statues for the Northampton

73 Because medieval sculpture was often integral to the building the sculptor's role could never be precisely differentiated from other aspects of masonry. In a fourteenth-century work like the great screen at Southwell Minster it is hard to say where architecture ends and sculpture begins.

74 *Opposite* The subject matter of a great programme of sculptures on a building such as Wells Cathedral would be worked out by the clergy, but the patterns were probably supplied by the master mason.

75 *Left* The unfinished fourteenth-century reliefs on the façade of Orvieto Cathedral show several phases of work, from the roughed-out earlier stages to the highly finished details, such as foliage, wings and hair.

76 *Opposite top* Relief sculptures in the Lady Chapel at Ely, contemporaries of those at Orvieto, were done by at least six sculptors, each working all over the building.

77 and 78 *Opposite bottom* The Easter Sepulchres at Heckington, Lincolnshire (left), and Hawton, Nottinghamshire (right), were made in the fourteenth century to a similar design but by separate teams of sculptors.

Eleanor Cross were transported there ready-carved, as were some bosses for Exeter Cathedral in 1301/2, although three years later we find pre-carved capitals and bases being delivered to Exeter from Portland, together with '18 great stones . . . for bosses' which were then carved at 5 shillings each. At Orvieto the fitting of the relief slabs is so inept in places that they must have been marked out and mostly carved before they were set in the wall. The chancel fittings at Heckington and Hawton, however, were clearly measured and carved on the site, not acquired in pre-cut sections from the quarry. Capitals, bases and vault bosses seem to have been ordered when required rather than made in bulk; at Troyes in 1455 the mason Anthoine was even made to finish a capital that had been begun by an itinerant worker, but this may be yet another example of the decidedly chaotic conditions there.

Manuscript illuminations show sculptors carving foliage and figure sculpture. They normally worked on the ground, but we know from the Milan records that some carving was done on the scaffolding. In northern Europe figures were usually made of the same stone as the building (they were in any case painted over), but from the thirteenth century marble and alabaster were used for tomb effigies, and in the south, especially in Italy, sculptural embellishment was often in a different stone to add both contrast and a feeling of preciousness. The stone block was marked with chalk and the sculptor worked straight on to it. When the general shape had been roughed out and the draperies carved a figure was often hollowed out at the back to make it lighter. This would not show on a figure standing in a niche or against a wall, which would in addition be secured in position by metal ties.

The sculptor's tools were successively finer: he began with an axe or hammer, progressing to chisels and drills for the close work, before finishing the surface with a claw chisel and file. The reliefs at Orvieto, which were abandoned unfinished, show the carving in different stages, revealing both the methods of achieving certain effects and the concept as it developed in the designer's mind. The differ-

79 A stone figure to be set in a niche often had its back hollowed out to lighten its weight. This would be invisible to the spectator.

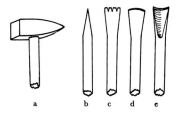

80 A selection of tools used in sculpture, each with its essential role in the stages between roughing out and the smooth finish. From left to right: trimming hammer; punch; claw-chisel; bull-nosed chisel; gouge.

reasonable parallel might be drawn with a painter's studio in which the master applied the finishing touches to a painting that had been largely executed by his assistants.

As so often with medieval art, it is difficult to find a comparison for Orvieto, so we can only infer that the Orvieto methods reflect common practice. That this kind of relief work was a team effort is beyond dispute, but the individuality of style from one place to another strongly indicates a powerful controlling intelligence directing work at each site. Where we know that the master mason was also a sculptor, we may be allowed to presume that the controlling intelligence was his. At Orvieto, however, the documents allow only a conjecture that the sculpture was designed and partly carved by Lorenzo Maitani, the *capomaestro* of the cathedral and a leading mason of his day. The late Middle Ages leave us with a teasing paradox: as the sculptor became independent of the building team and emerged as an artist in his own right, so did his art become ever closer to the architecture whence it came.

ent sized marble slabs and the many hands show that, as at Beverley, the planning was centrally controlled; this was particularly necessary with complicated narrative scenes, as from quite an early stage the scene ceased to be treated as a whole. Once it was roughly punched out, work began on the fine details, and any sense of the picture being carved evenly all over was lost. A few senior craftsmen may have been responsible for blocking out the entire scheme before their assistants attended to backgrounds, landscape details and architectural settings. These, especially the trees and decorative vine-scrolls, are all well advanced, while figures are often less so. There seem to have been specialist carvers of hair and wings, and they tried to make allowance for error by leaving a rim of stone round the head, which was cut away only when all work on the head was finished. The same kind of graded tools were used, and the final stages were in the hands of the most highly-skilled carvers. A

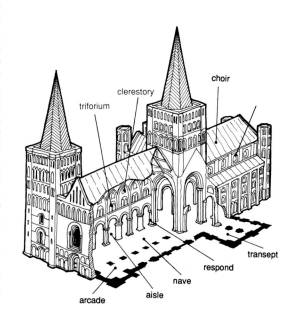

GLOSSARY

banker Workbench in the masons' lodge

caementarius Latin word for a mason

capomaestro (Lit: head master). Italian word for the master mason

centering Arched wooden framework upon which arches and vaults are built

chevet The east end of a church, comprising the choir and radiating chapels. Usually applied to the rounded, rather than the square, plan

chord Straight line drawn across a circle or arc

garderobe Lavatory

grillage Cross beams laid to form foundations

keystone Stone at the apex of an arch or meeting point of vault ribs

lathomus Latin term for a stone cutter

module Measure that sets a series of proportions in a building

mullion Vertical bar of stone dividing a window opening

orthogonal Line of projection perpendicular to the plane

putlog Scaffolding bar

Rayonnant Style of French Gothic architecture from *c.* 1240, named from the radiating patterns of the rose windows

respond A half-column or pilaster supporting an arch

retable Altarpiece

sedilia Priests' seats next to the altar

sleeper wall Foundation wall

springers Stones at the base of a vault from which the

ribs 'spring'

tas-de-charge Through stone, running the depth of the wall to convey the thrust of the vault to the exterior

triforium Arched passage, the middle storey of a Gothic elevation

voussoir Wedge-shaped stone forming part of an arch

FURTHER READING

The literature on all aspects of medieval masoncraft is extensive. The selection of publications given below includes both standard works and more recent books and articles that are particularly useful. Nearly all of them contain full bibliographies.

Documentary sources for the lives and careers of medieval masons and of medieval building will be found in:
H.M. COLVIN,
The History of the King's Works, vols I-III, The Middle Ages, London, 1963.
L.F. SALZMAN,
Building in England down to 1540, rev.edn, Oxford, 1967.
H.M. COLVIN, ed.,
Building Accounts of King Henry III, Oxford, 1971.
A. ERSKINE, ed.,
The Accounts of the Fabric of Exeter Cathedral, Devon and Cornwall Record Society, n.s. 24 (1981), 26 (1983).
J.H. HARVEY,
English Medieval Architects. A Bibliographical Dictionary down to 1550, rev. edn, Gloucester, 1984.

S. MURRAY,
Building Troyes Cathedral, Bloomington, 1987.
The best source for French material is still:
V. MORTET and P. DESCHAMPS, *Recueil des textes relatifs à l'histoire de l'architecture et à la condition des architectes en France au moyen age*, 2 vols, Paris 1911-28.

Contracts of Spanish masons are printed in:
G.E. STREET,
Some account of Gothic Architecture in Spain, ed. G.G. King, 2vols, London, 1914.

General works on building and builders, all with good bibliographies, include:
D. KNOOP and G.P. JONES,
The Medieval Mason, 3rd edn, Manchester,1967.
L.R. SHELBY,
'The role of the master mason in mediæval English building',
Speculum, xxxix (1964), pp. 387-403.
S. KOSTOF, ed.,
The Architect. Chapters in the History of the Profession, New York, 1977.
J. GIMPEL,
The Cathedral Builders, trans. Carl F. Barnes,Jr, New York, 1961.
P. COLOMBIER,
Les chantiers des cathédrales: ouvriers, architectes, sculpteurs, rev. edn, 1990
R. RECHT, ed.,
Les bâtisseurs des cathédrales gothiques, Strasbourg, 1989. Discusses French, German, Spanish and Italian material.

Valuable information on Germany is also given by
B. SCHOCK-WERNER and

others in
Die Parler und der schöne Stil 1350-1400, exhibition catalogue, ed. A. LEGNER, 5 vols, Cologne, Schnutgen Museum, 1978.

For tools and techniques see also:
Age of Chivalry, exhibition catalogue, ed. J. ALEXANDER and P. BINSKI, London, Royal Academy of Arts, 1987.

For design techniques see the above general works and:
L.R. SHELBY,
Gothic Design Techniques. The Fifteenth-century Design Booklets of Mathes Roriczer and Hanns Schmuttermayer, Carbondale, 1977.
J. ACKERMAN,
'"Ars sine Scientia nihil est": Gothic theory of architecture at the Cathedral of Milan', *Art Bulletin*, xxxi (1949), pp. 84-111.
F.B. TOKER,
'Gothic architecture by remote control: An illustrated contract of 1340', *Art Bulletin*, lxvii (1985), pp.67-95.

For techniques of sculpture see:
J. WHITE,
'The reliefs on the façade of the Duomo at Orvieto', *Journal of the Warburg and Courtauld Institutes*, xxxii (1959), pp.254-302.
The essays by V. SEKULES and N. DAWTON in:
F.H. THOMPSON ed., *Studies in Medieval Sculpture*, London, Society of Antiquaries, Occasional Paper (New Series), III, 1983
P. WILLIAMSON

Gothic Sculpture 1140-1300, New Haven and London, 1995.

PHOTOGRAPHIC CREDITS

The author and publishers are grateful to the following for permission to reproduce illustrations:

Arch. Phot. Paris/SPADEM: 50; Archivi Alinari SpA, Florence: 67, 75; Archives Municipales de Strasbourg (Photo: E. Laemmel): 5; Carl F. Barnes Jr. © Bibliothèque Nationale, Paris: 31 (MS lat. 11560, fol. 55r); The Bath and Portland Stone Company, Bath: 26; Bayerisches Staatsbibliothek, Munich: 59 (Cod. Germ.5, fol. 29); Bibliothèque Nationale, Paris: 1 (MS fr. 247, fol. 163), 12 (MS lat. 11560, fol. 35v), 17 (MS lat. 4915, fol. 46v); Bibliothèque Royale Albert 1er, Brussels: 8 (MS 6, fol. 554v); Bildarchiv Foto Marburg/Lahn: 4, 15, 44, 74; Bildarchiv Preussischer Kulturbesitz, Berlin: 32, 53; Drawings by Susan Bird. © British Museum Press: 36 and 37 (after Professor Eric Fernie), 38, 40, 45, 52, 64,p.70 (right); Board of Trinity College, Dublin: 9 (TCD 177, fol. 59v); Drawing by John Atherton Bowen: 48; British Library, London: title page (MS Cotton Aug. AV, fol. 51v), 2 (Add MS 47682, fol. 2), back cover and 6 (Add MS 18850, fol. 554v), 10 (MS Cotton Nero D1, fol. 23v), 46 (Cotton Aug. AV, fol. 22), 54 (Add 35313, fol. 34), 58 (MS Egerton 1894, fol. 5v); Burgerbibliothek, Bern: 43 (MSS hist. helv. I, 16, p.81); Caisse Nationale des Monuments Historiques et des Sites/SPADEM, Paris (Photo: Jean Feuille): 16; Cliché Fortin © 1971 Inventaire Général/SPADEM: 30; Nicola Coldstream: 61; Conway Library, London. © Courtauld Institute: 22, 23, 28, 33, 39, 56, 68, 76, 77, 78; Conway Library, London. © Canon M. H.

INDEX